The
Rational emotive
behavioural
approach to therapeutic change

Sage Therapeutic Change Series

Books in the *Sage Therapeutic Change Series* examine 'change' as the goal of counselling and psychotherapy. Each book takes a different therapeutic approach and looks at how change is conceptualised and worked with by practitioners from that approach. Giving examples which demonstrate how theory and principles are put into practice, the books are suitable for both trainee and experienced counsellors and psychotherapists.

Series Editor: Windy Dryden

Books in the series:

The Rational Emotive Behavioural Approach to Therapeutic Change
Windy Dryden & Michael Neenan

'A remarkably useful book for the practitioners of Rational Emotive Behaviour Therapy and other kinds of Cognitive Behaviour Therapy. Very clearly and intensively covers what effective therapeutic change is and the therapist's and the client's role in following it and in fighting against relapsing. Dryden and Neenan's book includes many important points that are often omitted from REBT and other therapies. Definitive and thoroughgoing!' – **Albert Ellis, President of Albert Ellis Institute**.

The Psychodynamic Approach to Therapeutic Change
Rob Leiper & Michael Maltby

The Person-Centred Approach to Therapeutic Change
Michael McMillan

The
Rational emotive
behavioural
approach to therapeutic change

Windy Dryden &
Michael Neenan

SAGE Publications
London • Thousand Oaks • New Delhi

First published 2004

SAGE Publications Ltd
Olivers Yard
London EC1Y 1SP

SAGE Publications Inc.
2455 Teller Road
Thousand Oaks, California 91320

SAGE Publications India Pvt Ltd
B-42, Panchsheel Enclave
Post Box 4109
New Delhi 100 017

British Library Cataloguing in Publication data

A catalogue record for this book is available from the British
Library

ISBN 0 7619 4895 3
ISBN 0 7619 4869 1 (pbk)

Library of Congress Control Number: 2003108064

Typeset by C&M Digitals (P) Ltd, Chennai, India
Printed in Great Britain by TJ International Ltd, Padstow, Cornwall

Contents

List of Figures   vii

Introduction   1

1   The ABCs of Rational Emotive Behaviour Therapy   5

2   Different Types of Change   17

3   The REBT Change Sequence   35

4   The Role of the Therapist   46

5   The Role of the Client   67

6   Client Obstacles and How to Address Them   80

7   Therapist Obstacles and How to Address Them   93

8   Client–Therapist Obstacles and How to Address Them   108

9   The Process of Change   121

References   137

Index   141

List of Figures

1.1 As: examples of actual and inferred events – past, present and future 5

1.2 As: examples of actual and inferred events – external and internal 6

1.3 As: examples of situational As, critical As and non-critical inferred As – past, present and future 6

1.4 As: examples of situational As, critical As and non-critical inferred As – external and internal 7

1.5 Negative emotions, beliefs and inferential themes 13

1.6 Negative emotions and actions/action tendencies that stem from irrational and rational beliefs 14

1.7 Negative emotions and thinking consequences of irrational and rational beliefs 15

2.1 Changing an unhealthy negative emotion by changing one's critical A 19

4.1 Combinations of belief–behaviour–thinking configurations with their power to facilitate psychotherapeutic generalisation listed in descending order 65

In this book we will outline a view of psychotherapeutic change from the perspective of Rational Emotive Behaviour Therapy, an approach to cognitive-behaviour therapy that was originated in 1955 by Dr Albert Ellis, an American clinical psychologist. Ellis was previously a psycho-analyst who became disenchanted with the effectiveness and efficiency of psychoanalysis and psychoanalytic psychotherapy. After a brief experimental period with different therapeutic methods of the day, Ellis crystallised his ideas on therapy into an integrative approach which he named 'Rational Therapy'. This approach was based on a number of principles which still form the basis of REBT today, as outlined below.

Cognitions are important to an understanding of the way people feel and act

This principle has its roots in Stoic philosophy in general, and in particular the writings of Epictetus, who has been credited with this cognitive conceptualisation of psychological disturbance: 'Men are disturbed not by things, but by their views of things.' REBT's current position on this point can be summed up in the following version of Epictetus' saying: 'People are disturbed not by things, but by their rigid and extreme views of things.'

Cognitions, emotions and behaviours are not separate psychological processes, but often interact in complex ways

From the outset, Ellis adhered to the principle of psychological interactionism which states that cognitions, emotions and behaviours are interdependent processes. Ellis has, of late, acknowledged that it was a mistake to call his therapeutic approach 'Rational Therapy', for two reasons. First, the name suggested that the approach *only* focused on cognitions; and second, by not mentioning emotions and behaviours it did not prepare professionals who were new to the approach, or clients of the approach, for an integrative view of the latter's psychological problems. The current name of the approach, 'Rational Emotive Behaviour Therapy', corrects both of these mistakes.

Cognitive and emotive change is facilitated by behavioural change

From the beginning, Ellis held that if people act on their developing rational beliefs they are more likely to make appropriate cognitive and emotive changes, and if they do not act on these beliefs, they minimise the chances that such changes will be made. This position has remained the same ever since. In fact, REBT without a decided behavioural emphasis is like cognition without ignition.

Therapists in REBT serve their clients best by taking an active–directive approach to help de-propagandise the irrational ideas that they hold about themselves, other people and the world

At the outset, Ellis stressed that people make themselves disturbed by the irrational ideas (now beliefs) they hold about themselves, other people and the world. He also stressed that, when disturbed, people frequently cling on to these irrational beliefs. It follows, Ellis argued, that REBT therapists need to take an active–directive stance in helping their clients identify such irrational ideas and so help them de-propagandise these ideas. While the terminology of 'de-propagandise' is no longer used by Ellis or other REBT therapists, it does highlight the fact that Ellis encourages REBT therapists to actively help their client be strongly critical of their irrational beliefs.

The term 'propaganda' also suggests that the client has uncritically accepted one or more irrational ideas that lie at the core of his or her disturbed feelings. While most people think of propaganda as coming from outside the person (e.g. from one's parents, peers, the media, etc.) – and Ellis' early writing did stress these as the likely sources of such propaganda – it is possible to think of such propaganda as coming from within the person. Thus, Ellis' later writings place more emphasis on the person as the main source of his own irrational ideas and as actively propagandising himself with these ideas. Thus, while a person may learn from a variety of outside sources that approval is very desirable, he is the one who constructs an irrational idea about this desirable commodity and subsequently disturbs himself with the thought of not gaining approval ('Because it is desirable for me to gain approval, I absolutely must do so'). He is the one who creates such unhealthy propaganda for himself and keeps it alive in a number of ways. Even when the dogmatic propaganda comes from outside the person (such as when a teacher tells a pupil 'You must do well in your exams and it will be terrible if you don't'), it is only disturbing when he uncritically accepts such external dogmatic propaganda and makes it his own internal dogmatic propaganda ('Yes, you are right, I must do well in my exams and it will be terrible if I don't').

When other people encourage the person to think in dogmatic ways, he has the choice to reject this encouragement. Thus, in response to the example above the person could say: 'You say that I must do well in my exams and it would be terrible if I don't. However, you are wrong. I don't have to do well in my exams, although it would be desirable if I do so. And while it would be disadvantageous if I don't do well it wouldn't be terrible.' While this example demonstrates that it is possible for clients to be sceptical of external propaganda – and indeed of their own internal propaganda – they usually need quite a bit of help from their therapists to identify, challenge and change their irrational beliefs. The language of 'therapists helping clients to de-propagandise themselves against their irrational ideas' has been replaced by the language of 'therapists helping them to identify, challenge and change their irrational beliefs'. We will discuss this process more fully in Chapter 4.

While it is important that therapists empathise with their clients, show them respect and are congruent, these therapeutic conditions are neither necessary nor sufficient for therapeutic change to occur

All approaches to psychotherapy hold that the relationship between therapist and client is an important vehicle for client therapeutic change, although different approaches place differential weight on this relationship to promote such change. In 1959, Ellis published a response to Carl Rogers' (1957) seminal article in which the latter claimed that there were a number of therapeutic conditions necessary and sufficient for therapeutic change to occur. An up-to-date list of such conditions details empathy, unconditional positive regard and congruence. Ellis (1959) argued that while such conditions may well be useful in promoting therapeutic change, they are neither necessary nor sufficient for such change to occur. In part, this is consistent with Ellis' non-dogmatic view about any phenomena, but in the main it accords with his view that for therapeutic change to occur and be maintained, clients need to demonstrate an ongoing commitment to identifying, challenging and changing their irrational beliefs by using a variety of cognitive, emotive and behavioural techniques. It may well be that exposure to the aforementioned therapeutic conditions may encourage clients to make and act on this commitment, but it could also be that such exposure may *dis*courage clients from doing the hard work needed to promote and maintain therapeutic change. The client may feel better as a result of the experience of being understood and positively regarded by his therapist and therefore may not be motivated to get better by doing the hard work of change. The role that the therapeutic conditions have in promoting or discouraging client change in REBT awaits full empirical enquiry.

Current REBT theory draws upon working alliance theory to conceptualise the role that the therapeutic relationship has in fostering client change (Dryden, 1999). The therapeutic conditions put forward by Rogers and reconceptualised by REBT therapists as empathy, unconditional acceptance and genuineness are generally seen as part of the bond domain of the working alliance (Bordin, 1979). We discuss the role of the working alliance in promoting client change in Chapter 4.

Clients need to adopt a protestant ethic approach to therapeutic change

From the inception of REBT, Ellis stressed that if clients are going to achieve lasting change they will have to work hard to achieve and maintain such change. This is what we refer to as the protestant ethic approach to change. As we discuss in Chapter 6, one of the biggest obstacles to client change is the reluctance to acknowledge and/or implement this clinical reality. Indeed, one of the most important skills that an REBT therapist needs to acquire and develop is helping clients to overcome their resistance towards working for lasting change.

Let us briefly summarise what we are going to cover in this book. In Chapter 1, we present REBT's ABC model of psychological disturbance and change. In particular, we discuss the differences between rational and irrational beliefs. In Chapter 2, we outline the REBT view that there are different – albeit overlapping – types of client change. We briefly outline these different types of change before concentrating on the one that is seen by REBT as the most far-reaching, yielding the greatest gains for the individual concerned, namely belief change. While our focus throughout this book is on client change within the therapeutic setting, much of what we have to say is relevant to personal change outside of this context, and in Chapter 3 we consider the REBT change sequence and outline in order the steps that clients need to take to promote psychological change. The steps in this sequence are not prescriptive, but rather are descriptive of an ideal change sequence. Then in Chapters 4 and 5 we consider the respective roles of therapist and client in promoting client change. Chapters 6, 7 and 8 focus on obstacles to client change from three perspectives. In Chapter 6 we consider in detail the major obstacles to client change within the client, while in Chapter 7 we consider the obstacles that reside in the therapist, and in Chapter 8 we consider the main obstacles to client change that arise from the interaction between client and therapist. In each of these three chapters we consider ways that therapists can deal with these obstacles. Finally, in Chapter 9, we close the book with a discussion of the process of change in REBT.

In this chapter we will outline some basic principles of REBT, without an understanding of which it is unlikely that you will grasp the points we will be making about the different types of psychotherapeutic change discussed in the next chapter. These principles are enshrined in REBT's ABC model. From a clinical point of view, this model states that people are not disturbed at C in the ABC model by the events in their lives at A. Rather, they disturb themselves largely because of the beliefs that they hold about these events at B in the model.

Let us make a few important points arising from this model before discussing the different types of client change.

As

Traditionally in REBT theory, activating events at A about which we disturb ourselves can be actual or inferred events. An inference is a cognitive hunch about reality which may or may not be true, but which needs to be checked against the available evidence. As can refer to events in the past, the present or anticipations of the future. They can also refer to events external or internal to the person. Figures 1.1 and 1.2 provide examples of As.

Figure 1.1   As: examples of actual and inferred events – past, present and future

	Past	Present	Future
Actual A	My mother didn't buy me anything for my 14th birthday	My boss has just rung and asked to see me at the end of the day	Next week I will give an important presentation at work
Inferred A	My mother didn't care enough to buy me something for my 14th birthday	My boss has asked to see me because he is unhappy with my work	My presentation next week will be poor and people at work will sneer at me

REBT theory holds that when we disturb ourselves about an event, we are usually disturbing ourselves about a particular aspect of the event.

Figure 1.2   As: examples of actual and inferred events – external and internal

	External	Internal
Actual A	When I went into the room, Sarah walked out	I have been having headaches recently
Inferred A	Sarah walking out of the room when I walked in means that she doesn't like me	The headaches mean that I have a brain tumour

This aspect is known in REBT as the critical A. It is now our practice to distinguish between the critical A and the situational A in which the critical A is to be found. Note that what we have previously referred to as an actual A is now referred to as a situational A. Let us now re-present Figures 1.1 and 1.2, showing this distinction. In these figures (Figures 1.3 and 1.4), we will assume that inferred As are critical. Not *all* inferred As are critical of course, and to demonstrate this we will add a new row to show possible non-critical inferred As. These refer to other inferences that you can make about the situation at hand which you are *not* most disturbed about.

Figure 1.3   As: examples of situational As, critical As and non-critical inferred As – past, present and future

	Past	Present	Future
Situational A	My mother didn't buy me anything for my 14th birthday	My boss has just rung and asked to see me at the end of the day	Next week I will give an important presentation at work
Critical A	My mother didn't care enough to buy me something for my 14th birthday	My boss has asked to see me because he is unhappy with my work	My presentation next week will be poor and people at work will sneer at me
Non-critical inferred A	My mother was too ill to remember dates. That's why she didn't buy me a birthday present	My boss wants my advice about a job-related matter	My presentation next week will be poor, but people will understand that I am under pressure and couldn't do a better job

In REBT, when dealing with our clients' emotional problems we usually encourage them to assume temporarily that their critical As are true even though they appear to be distorted. Adopting this strategy helps us to

Figure 1.4 As: examples of situational As, critical As and non-critical inferred As – external and internal

	External	Internal
Situational A	When I went into the room, Sarah walked out	I have been having headaches recently
Critical A	Sarah walking out of the room when I walked in means that she doesn't like me	The headaches mean that I have a brain tumour
Non-critical inferred A	Sarah went to the toilet	The headaches mean that I am under stress and need to take it easy

identify the underlying irrational beliefs that underpin our clients' problems. If we challenged their critical As at this point and helped them to see, for example, that their alternative non-critical inferred As were a more accurate inferential representation of the situational A, we might help them not to feel disturbed, but we would be doing so by helping them to change the inferential meaning of the event rather than to change their irrational beliefs about the original inferential meaning. As we will see later in this book, REBT therapists consider belief change to be more far-reaching than inferential change, but because we are flexible in our practice and pragmatic in our aims, we may, at times, settle for inferential change when we think that the client may not be able to entertain belief change.

Bs

In REBT, B stands for 'beliefs', a term that is used in a particular way. Beliefs are deemed to be fully evaluative in nature and are either rational or irrational.

Irrational beliefs are evaluative ideas that have the following characteristics:

- They are rigid or extreme.
- They are inconsistent with reality.
- They are illogical or nonsensical.
- They yield largely dysfunctional consequences.

On the other hand, rational beliefs have the following characteristics:

- They are flexible or non-extreme.
- They are consistent with reality.

- They are logical or sensible.
- They yield largely functional consequences.

REBT theory posits four irrational beliefs and four rational alternatives.

Demands vs. non-dogmatic preferences

Demands

Demands are rigid ideas that people hold about how things absolutely must or must not be. Demands can be placed on oneself ('I must do well'), on others ('You must treat me well'), or on life conditions ('Life must be fair'). Ellis' view is that of all the irrational beliefs, it is these demands that are at the very core of psychological disturbance. The healthy alternative to a demand is a full preference.

Non-dogmatic preferences

Non-dogmatic preferences, by contrast, are flexible ideas that people hold about how they would like things to be without demanding that they have to be that way. Non-dogmatic preferences can relate to oneself ('I want to do well, but I don't have to do so'), to others ('I want you to treat me well, but unfortunately you don't have to do so'), or to life conditions ('I very much want life to be fair, but unfortunately it doesn't have to be the way I want it to be'). Again, Ellis' position is that of all the rational beliefs, it is these non-dogmatic preferences that are at the very core of psychological health.

Awfulising beliefs vs. non-awfulising beliefs

Awfulising beliefs

Awfulising beliefs are extreme ideas that people derive from their demands when these demands aren't met ('I must do well *and it's terrible if I don't*'; 'You must treat me well *and it's awful when you don't*'; and 'Life must be fair *and it's the end of the world when it's not*'). An awfulising belief stems from the demand that things must not be as bad as they are and is extreme in the sense that the person believes at the time one or more of the following:

- Nothing could be worse.
- The event in question is worse than 100 per cent bad.
- No good could possibly come from this bad event.

The healthy alternative to an awfulising belief is a non-awfulising belief.

Non-awfulising beliefs

Non-awfulising beliefs, by contrast, are non-extreme ideas that people hold as derivatives from their non-dogmatic preferences when these non-dogmatic preferences aren't met ('I want to do well, but I don't have to do so. *It's bad if I don't do well, but not terrible'*; 'I want you to treat me well, but unfortunately you don't have to do so. *When you don't treat me well it's really unfortunate, but not awful'*, and 'I very much want life to be fair, but unfortunately it doesn't have to be the way I want it to be. *If life is unfair, that's very bad, but not the end of the world'*). A non-awfulising belief stems from the non-dogmatic preference that I'd like things not to be as bad as they are, but that doesn't mean that they must not be that bad, and is non-extreme in the sense that the person believes at the time one or more of the following:

- Things could always be worse.
- The event in question is less than 100 per cent bad.
- Good can come from this bad event.

Low frustration tolerance beliefs vs. high frustration tolerance beliefs

Low frustration tolerance beliefs

Low frustration tolerance beliefs are extreme ideas that people derive from their demands not being met ('I must do well *and I can't bear it if I don't'*; 'You must treat me well *and it's intolerable when you don't'*, and 'Life must be fair *and I can't stand it when it's not'*). A low frustration tolerance belief stems from the demand that things must not be as frustrating or uncomfortable as they are, and is extreme in the sense that at the time the person believes one or more of the following:

- I will die or disintegrate if the frustration or discomfort continues to exist.
- I will lose the capacity to experience happiness if the frustration or discomfort continues to exist.
- The frustration or discomfort is not worth tolerating.

The healthy alternative to a low frustration tolerance belief is a high frustration tolerance belief.

High frustration tolerance beliefs

High frustration beliefs, by contrast, are non-extreme ideas that people derive from their non-dogmatic preferences when these non-dogmatic preferences aren't met ('I want to do well, but I don't have to do so. *When I don't do well it is difficult to bear, but I can bear it and it's worth bearing'*; 'I want you to treat me well, but unfortunately you don't have to do so. *When you don't treat me well it's really hard to tolerate, but I can tolerate it and it's worth it to me to do so'*, and 'I very much want life to be fair, but unfortunately it doesn't have to be the way I want it to be. *If life is unfair, that's hard to stand, but I can stand it and it is in my best interests to do so'*). A high frustration tolerance belief stems from the non-dogmatic preference that it is undesirable when things are as frustrating or uncomfortable as they are, but unfortunately things don't have to be different. It is non-extreme in the sense that the person at the time believes one or more of the following:

- I will struggle if the frustration or discomfort continues to exist, but I will neither die nor disintegrate.
- I will not lose the capacity to experience happiness if the frustration or discomfort continues to exist, although this capacity will be temporarily diminished.
- The frustration or discomfort is worth tolerating.

Depreciation vs. acceptance beliefs

Depreciation beliefs

Depreciation beliefs are extreme ideas that people hold about self, other(s) and the world. These beliefs derive from their demands not being met ('I must do well and I am a failure it if I don't'; 'You must treat me well and you are a bad person if you don't', and 'Life must be fair and the world is bad if it isn't'). A depreciation belief stems from the demand that I, you, or things must be as I want them to be and is extreme in the sense that the person believes at the time one or more of the following:

- A person can legitimately be given a single global rating that defines them, and one's worth is dependent upon conditions that change ('My worth goes up when I do well and goes down when I don't do well').
- The world can legitimately be given a single rating that defines it and the value of the world varies according to what happens within it (the value of the world goes up when something fair occurs and goes down when something unfair happens).
- A person can be rated on the basis of one of his or her aspects.
- The world can be rated on the basis of one of its aspects.

The healthy alternative to a depreciation belief is an acceptance belief.

Acceptance beliefs

Acceptance beliefs, by contrast, are non-extreme ideas that people derive from their non-dogmatic preferences when these non-dogmatic preferences aren't met ('I want to do well, but I don't have to do so. *When I don't do well I am not a failure. I am a fallible human being who is not doing well on this occasion*'; 'I want you to treat me well, but unfortunately you don't have to do so. *When you don't treat me well, you are not a bad person, rather a fallible human being who is treating me poorly*', and 'I very much want life to be fair, but unfortunately it doesn't have to be the way I want it to be.

If life is unfair it is only unfair in this respect and doesn't prove that the world is a rotten place. The world is a complex place where many good, bad and neutral things happen'). An acceptance belief is non-extreme in the sense that the person believes at the time one or more of the following:

- A person cannot legitimately be given a single global rating that defines them and their worth. It is not dependent upon conditions that change ('My worth stays the same whether or not I do well').
- The world cannot legitimately be given a single rating that defines its essential nature. The value of the world does not vary according to what happens within it (the value of the world stays the same whether fairness exists or not).
- It makes sense to rate discrete aspects of a person and of the world, but it does not make sense to rate a person or the world on the basis of these discrete aspects.

Cs

In REBT, 'C' refers to the consequences of the beliefs held at B. There are three sets of consequences: emotional, behavioural and cognitive, and it is important to consider each in the change process.

Emotional Cs

REBT has an intriguing view about emotional consequences of beliefs at B. When a client holds an irrational belief about a critical A, he will experience an unhealthy negative emotion at C. However, if he holds a rational belief about the same event, he will experience a healthy negative emotion at C. This means that REBT has a qualitative view of emotions rather than the more commonly found quantitative view.

Let us briefly outline the major difference between these two views with reference to anxiety. The quantitative view of anxiety is that it is a unitary response to threat, with strong levels deemed to be unhealthy when there is no objective evidence for the existence of the threat. Moderate and mild levels of anxiety are also deemed to be somewhat inappropriate in the absence of threat, but this is seen as less problematic. When threat exists, anxiety is deemed to be an appropriate response with the level of intensity matching the size of the threat. By contrast, the qualitative view of anxiety contrasts this emotion with concern, with the former stemming from irrational beliefs about the threat and the latter stemming from rational beliefs about the same threat. According to this view, both anxiety and concern vary in intensity, but all levels of anxiety are unhealthy because they stem from irrational beliefs, whereas all levels of concern are healthy because they stem from rational beliefs. Furthermore, the qualitative view holds that people make distorted inferences about threat because of their implicit irrational beliefs, whereas they make realistic inferences of threat when their implicit beliefs are rational. The major therapeutic difference between these two views becomes clear when we consider a client's response to a sizeable objectively existing threat. The quantitative view holds that a strong level of anxiety is appropriate under these circumstances, whereas the qualitative view holds that a strong level of concern is appropriate, but a strong level of anxiety is unhealthy.

REBT therapists are primarily concerned with helping their clients overcome eight unhealthy negative emotions. Figure 1.5 lists these emotions and shows which emotion is experienced about which inferential theme. Also listed are the alternative healthy negative emotions. There are two points to note here: firstly, as we highlighted above, unhealthy negative emotions stem from irrational beliefs, while healthy negative emotions stem from rational beliefs; and secondly, both sets of emotions are experienced in reaction to same theme. Inferential themes do not explain whether negative emotions are healthy or unhealthy; on the other hand, the rationality or irrationality of the beliefs held about these themes do. Please note that Figure 1.5 does not show all possible inferential themes related to each emotional pairing, only the major ones.

Behavioural Cs

In keeping with its qualitative view of consequences at C, REBT argues that the behavioural consequences of rational beliefs tend to be constructive in nature, whereas the behavioural consequences of irrational beliefs tend to be unconstructive in nature. Now, REBT differentiates between two types of behavioural consequences: actual behaviours and action tendencies – the latter representing an urge to act in a certain way which is not transformed into overt behaviour. As we will see later on, an important part of the change process involves the client refraining from acting on unconstructive action tendencies and instead acting in ways that are consistent with constructive action tendencies.

Figure 1.6 outlines a sample of the most common action tendencies and overt behaviours associated with the irrational beliefs and rational beliefs underpinning each of the unhealthy and healthy negative emotions respectively.

Cognitive Cs

The final set of consequences that we wish to discuss are cognitive in nature. REBT theory hypothesises that when a client holds an irrational belief, his subsequent thinking is more likely to be distorted than when he

Figure 1.5   Negative emotions, beliefs and inferential themes

Inferential theme	Belief	Unhealthy negative emotion	Healthy negative emotion
Threat	Irrational	Anxiety	
Threat	Rational		Concern
Loss, failure	Irrational	Depression	
Loss, failure	Rational		Sadness
Transgression of rule	Irrational	Unhealthy anger	
Transgression of rule	Rational		Healthy anger
Moral lapse, hurting others	Irrational	Guilt	
Moral lapse, hurting others	Rational		Remorse
Undeserved treatment from significant other	Irrational	Hurt	
Undeserved treatment from significant other	Rational		Sorrow
Revealing that one has fallen short of ideal	Irrational	Shame	
Revealing that one has fallen short of ideal	Rational		Disappointment
Threat to relationship	Irrational	Unhealthy jealousy	
Threat to relationship	Rational		Healthy jealousy
Coveting something that another has but one lacks	Irrational	Unhealthy envy	
Coveting something that another has but one lacks	Rational		Healthy envy

holds a rational belief. In a series of studies, colleagues and I (WD) have tested this hypothesis and found a great deal of support for it (Bond & Dryden, 1996, for example).

Figure 1.7 outlines a sample of the most common thinking consequences of the irrational beliefs and rational beliefs underpinning each of the unhealthy and healthy negative emotions respectively.

Figure 1.6   Negative emotions and actions/action tendencies that stem from irrational and rational beliefs

Belief	Unhealthy negative emotion	Healthy negative emotion	Action tendency and/or overt behaviour
Irrational	Anxiety		Avoiding or withdrawing from the threat
Rational		Concern	Confronting and dealing with the threat
Irrational	Depression		Withdrawing from others into self
Rational		Sadness	Communicating feelings to others
Irrational	Unhealthy anger		Attacking others verbally/physically
Rational		Healthy anger	Asserting self with others
Irrational	Guilt		Begging for forgiveness
Rational		Remorse	Asking for forgiveness
Irrational	Hurt		Sulking
Rational		Sorrow	Communicating openly with the other
Irrational	Shame		Averting one's eyes
Rational		Disappointment	Maintaining eye contact with the other
Irrational	Unhealthy jealousy		Questioning partner with suspicion, but without foundation
Rational		Healthy jealousy	Questioning partner without suspicion only when relevant
Irrational	Unhealthy envy		Desperately trying to obtain coveted object
Rational		Healthy envy	Non-desperately trying to obtain coveted object only if one truly wants it

Figure 1.7 Negative emotions and thinking consequences of irrational and rational beliefs

Belief	Unhealthy negative emotion	Healthy negative emotion	Thinking consequences
Irrational	Anxiety		Overestimating negative consequences of the threat
Rational		Concern	Realistic appraisal of negative consequences of the threat
Irrational	Depression		Overly negative view of the future
Rational		Sadness	Realistic view of the future
Irrational	Unhealthy anger		Thoughts of revenge
Rational		Healthy anger	Thoughts of assertion
Irrational	Guilt		Assumes more personal responsibility than the situation warrants
Rational		Remorse	Assumes appropriate level of personal responsibility
Irrational	Hurt		Thinks that other must make first move
Rational		Sorrow	Thinks about how best to express feelings to the other
Irrational	Shame		Thinks that everyone is judging one negatively
Rational		Disappointment	Thinks that one will get a range of reactions from people: critical, neutral and compassionate
Irrational	Unhealthy jealousy		Is distrustful of anything that partner says
Rational		Healthy jealousy	Is trustful, but healthily sceptical of what partner says
Irrational	Unhealthy envy		Thinks of ways of getting coveted object, no matter what
Rational		Healthy envy	Thinks of ways of getting coveted object, only if it will have lasting value and the pursuit is not self-defeating

As, Bs and Cs interact

REBT puts forward an interdependent view of human psychological processes. This means that it argues that pure cognition, pure emotion and pure behaviour do not – in all probability – exist. Rather, cognition, emotion and behaviour are related to one another in often complex ways. This is an important point to bear in mind later in this book when we consider the nature of belief change.

Having introduced you to the basics of REBT theory, in the next chapter we discuss the different types of psychotherapeutic change considered by REBT therapists.

In this chapter we consider different types of change. You will notice that we did not use the term 'psychotherapeutic change' here. We chose our words carefully for a very good reason. Not all types of change are therapeutic. REBT theory argues that belief change is the healthiest, most elegant and most enduring form of client change and as such we will focus on this form of change in the main body of this book. This form of change is mainly psychotherapeutic. In a nutshell, belief change involves a client modifying his rigid and extreme (i.e. irrational) beliefs and internalising a set of alternative flexible and non-extreme (i.e. rational) beliefs. However, REBT also recognises that there are other forms of change in addition to belief change. In this chapter, we will consider these other forms before returning to belief change. These types of change can be therapeutic, but they can also lead to non-therapeutic consequences. Finally, we will discuss REBT's interdependence principle of change.

Inferential change

Inferential change occurs when a person changes the inferences that he makes at A without making a concomitant change in belief. As an example, consider the case of Mark who felt hurt when he inferred that his lecturer ignored him at an art gallery. Looking at this episode within an ABC framework we have:

Situational A = I saw my lecturer at the local art gallery and he did not acknowledge me.

Critical A = My lecturer ignored me.

Irrational B = He absolutely should not have ignored me and it's terrible that he did. Poor me!

C = Hurt

For Mark to have made a belief change, he would first have to assume that his critical inference at A was true and then change his belief at B. However, he did not do this. Rather, he overheard his lecturer later mentioning that he had an eye infection and was using eye drops and was only at the art gallery because his daughter wanted to go. On hearing this, Mark changed his critical inference from: 'My lecturer ignored me at the local art gallery' to 'My lecturer did not ignore me at the local art gallery. He had drops in his eye and probably did not recognise me or even see me because of this.' As a result, Mark stopped feeling hurt, not by changing his irrational belief at B but, as shown above, by changing his inference at A (see below; the italicised sections outline what Mark did subsequently and the effects of his actions).

Situational A = I saw my lecturer at the local art gallery and he did not acknowledge me.
Mark still held that this was true.

Critical A = My lecturer ignored me.
On hearing that his lecturer was suffering from an eye infection and had drops in his eyes, Mark changed his inference to: 'My lecturer did not ignore me at the local art gallery. He had drops in his eyes and probably did not recognise me or even see me because of this.'

Irrational B = He absolutely should not have ignored me and it's terrible that he did. Poor me!
Because Mark changed his inference at A and no longer thought that his lecturer had ignored him, there was no reason for him to hold an irrational belief at B.

C = Hurt
Given that he no longer held an irrational belief, he no longer felt hurt. He also had no reason to feel sorrowful (the healthy alternative to hurt).

Figure 2.1 shows, in diagrammatic form, inferential change.

Figure 2.1   Changing an unhealthy negative emotion by changing one's critical A

Situational A	*Situational A*
The situation in which the person disturbed himself	Remains the same
Critical A	*New A*
The person sees the situational A in relation to his personal domain (e.g. a threat to it, a loss from it, etc.) and makes an inference which triggers his irrational belief at B	The person makes a different inference which does not impact so centrally on his personal domain. The situation no longer constitutes, for example, a threat to or a loss from the personal domain
Irrational B	*New B relates to new A*
The person holds an irrational belief about this critical A	Because the person has changed his critical A, he ceases to hold his irrational belief. He develops a new B about his new A
Emotion	*New emotion*
Unhealthy negative emotion	The person's new emotion will stem from his new A and B

Because people are reluctant to change their beliefs when they can easily change their inferences, an important strategy in REBT practice is to encourage clients to assume temporarily that their inferences at A are true, even if they are clearly distorted. This gives your clients an opportunity to change their irrational beliefs, which remain activated, as long as they think their inferences are true. Thus, the problem with inferential change is that it shuts down opportunities for belief change. From Mark's perspective, why should he work on changing his irrational belief about being ignored when he has clear evidence that he was not ignored? Unless he understands why it is in his long-term interests to change his irrational belief, he will not do so because inferential change got rid of his feelings of hurt very quickly in this situation, a faster solution to his immediate painful feelings of hurt than the more durable, but time-consuming process of challenging and changing irrational beliefs.

Another reason that your clients may well be more motivated in the shorter term to change their inferences at A than to change their irrational beliefs at B, is that inference change often involves the client taking the negativity out of his inferences and offers him a more benign explanation of the situational A. In Mark's example, his situational A was, if you recall, 'I saw my lecturer at the local art gallery and he did not acknowledge me.' His original inference was 'My lecturer ignored me.' He then changed this inference on the basis of new information to 'My lecturer did not ignore me at the local art gallery. He had drops in his eye and probably did not recognise me or even me because of this.' As you can see, this inference is more benign and some clients will be persuaded by such a benign inference and not want to face up to the more negative inference. If they are to do so, the therapist will need to give a persuasive rationale for doing this.

Similarly, a client may be prepared to accept an inference that is less negative than his original critical A rather than face up to the greater aversiveness in the critical A itself, and then to work at identifying and changing his irrational belief. An example of this would be Mark accepting the inference that his lecturer has a general policy of not acknowledging students outside the university campus, rather than facing up to the greater aversiveness of his original critical A: that his lecturer ignored *him*. Once again, when the client changes his inference to one less aversive than his original critical A, his irrational belief is not triggered and although he has removed his unhealthy negative emotion quite quickly, he has lost an opportunity to achieve a more durable result by focusing on and changing his irrational belief in the face of an aversive critical inference.

Other clients won't be prepared to accept benign or less negative inferences and this is a sign that their irrational beliefs are fairly well entrenched. If this was the case with Mark, and you were trying to work with him inferentially by encouraging him to stand back and examine the validity of his critical A, the strength of his irrational belief, 'My lecturer must show that he likes me all the time', would prevent him from entertaining the greater validity of the two alternative inferential explanations of the lecturer's behaviour, namely i) his lecturer had an eye infection and didn't see him, and ii) his lecturer has a general policy of not acknowledging students off campus.

In this case, Mark's irrational belief would lead him to pick holes in the two alternative explanations. When considering the inference that his lecturer did not see him because the lecturer had an eye infection, Mark would conclude that if his lecturer's eye infection was that bad then he would not have attended the art gallery. Then, on being told that his lecturer had a general policy of not acknowledging students off campus, Mark would conclude that lecturers generally say this, but in practice they do acknowledge students when they come face-to-face with them. What is happening here is that the force of Mark's irrational belief leads him to make the inference that his lecturer had ignored him and to find holes in the two plausible-sounding alternative inferences. The advantage to you as an REBT therapist in this situation is that because Mark will only accept the truth of his inference that his lecturer ignored him at the art gallery, you will be able to use this as a gateway to helping him first to identify his irrational belief that largely determines his feelings of hurt, and thence to challenge and change it. As we said earlier, if Mark accepted either of the two alternative inferences, he would be far less motivated to assume that his original critical A was true as a means of helping him to work towards belief change.

In the practice of REBT, strategies designed to effect inferential change are implemented when it becomes clear that the client does not respond well to concerted efforts to bring about belief change. However, sometimes inferential change may promote belief change. To illustrate this point, let's suppose that Mark discussed the incident where he felt hurt about being ignored by his lecturer at the local art gallery with his REBT therapist. His therapist would have encouraged Mark to assume temporarily that his critical A ('My lecturer ignored me') was true, as a way of encouraging Mark to address the core of his hurt feelings, i.e. his irrational beliefs. Let's suppose that Mark did this, but was steadfast in his opposition to his therapist's attempts to encourage him to change his irrational belief to its rational alternative, and so change his unhealthy negative feelings of hurt to healthy negative feelings of sorrow or disappointment. As a result, Mark's therapist changed tack and questioned his critical A, and after examining the available evidence Mark reconsidered his critical A and, instead of thinking that his lecturer had ignored him, concluded that the man had not seen him due to having eye drops for an eye infection.

Having reconsidered his critical A and overcome his hurt feelings by making this inferential change, Mark was more responsive to going back and examining his irrational belief about his previous critical A (that his lecturer had ignored him).

Distracting oneself from the critical A

According to the REBT model, people disturb themselves about particular aspects of specific situations. As we have shown, these particular aspects are known as critical As.

In the previous section we discussed inference change, in which people change their unhealthy negative emotions by changing the inferences that comprise these critical As. Another way that people can change unhealthy negative emotions about their critical As is by distracting themselves from these As. For example, let's suppose that one of your clients has made himself anxious about an interview that he is to attend the following day. His ABC is as follows:

Situational A = I am to attend an interview tomorrow.

Critical A = I might not do well in the interview.

B = I must do well in the interview and if I don't it will prove that I am stupid.

C = Anxiety.

In order to get rid of his anxiety, your client distracts himself from thoughts of not doing well in the interview by listening to loud music. Again, note that this strategy brings about temporary emotional change, but the person remains vulnerable to anxiety because when he thinks again about not doing well in the interview (critical A) he is likely to feel anxious because of the irrational belief he holds at B.

Changing the situational A

Earlier (see pp. 5–6), we distinguished between a situational A and a critical A. The former represents the situational context in which your client experiences an unhealthy negative emotion and the latter is the aspect of the situational A about which the client is most disturbed. Your client can gain relief from his disturbed feelings by changing the situational A in a number of ways.

Perhaps the most obvious example of this type of change is where the client physically removes himself from the negative situational A in which he disturbed himself. Let's suppose, for example, that your client has made himself unhealthily angry about one of his co-workers' racist attitudes. One way of changing his dysfunctional anger is for your client to spend very little time in his co-worker's company. If this fails, a more drastic way of removing himself physically from the situational A would be for your client to change jobs. There are, of course, problems with such change strategies and particularly as a first-line therapeutic approach. For example, one can legitimately ask the question about such strategies:

what kind of change is being promoted? It is very unlikely that avoidance of negative life events will promote healthy and meaningful belief change. It is more likely to lead the person to learn that whenever one encounters a negative life event it is important to avoid it.

Another common approach to changing the situational A is making a direct modification to the activating event with the result that your client stops experiencing an unhealthy negative emotion. This involves your client confronting the situational A in order to change it, rather than avoiding it. An example of this approach is a client who makes himself unhealthily angry about his adolescent children playing music loudly on their hi-fi and who gets rid of his unhealthy angry feelings by taking the hi-fi away from his children so that they cannot play loud music. The problem with this direct approach to changing A is that it is often done under the influence of an unhealthy negative emotion and the person ends up reinforcing his irrational beliefs rather than changing them. In this case, the client changes the situational A in an unhealthy, angry way and in doing so – while he may have succeeded in getting rid of his unhealthy anger by confiscating the hi-fi – he has, in fact, reinforced the irrational belief that underpinned his unhealthy anger by acting in an unhealthy, angry manner.

There is nothing in REBT theory that is against direct modification of A, but we prefer that our clients first stop disturbing themselves about a situation, before changing it. We have this view because we argue that if someone is emotionally disturbed they are less likely to effect a constructive modification of the situational A than if they were experiencing a healthy negative emotion. For example, if your client is healthily angry about the noise that his children were making then he would more likely effect a constructive modification of this situational A than if he were unhealthily angry. Thus, if he were healthily angry, his first move would be to ask his children to turn the noise down, followed by healthy assertion, then by a clear, but non-aggressive statement of the logical consequences of not turning down the noise: that he will confiscate the hi-fi if the noise continues. If it does continue, your client would then modify the situation non-aggressively by confiscating the hi-fi. However, if he were unhealthily angry, your client would go straight to an aggressive modification of the situational A by aggressively taking the hi-fi away without any respectful attempt to assert himself with his children by stating clear boundaries for them.

You can see from this example that disturbed modification of the situational A may well quickly result in a change in the situation and that non-disturbed action may take more time. However, the latter often yields better long-term results. Thus, by taking action based on healthy anger rather than unhealthy anger, your client preserves in the longer term a respectful, but firmly boundaried relationship with his children and serves as a good role model for conflict resolution even though this route takes longer to reach his short-term objectives: a cessation of the noise. As we shall show throughout this book, therapeutic change involves putting up with short-term discomfort in order to achieve longer-term benefits.

This analysis strongly suggests that it is usually best to effect some measure of belief change before attempting to modify a problematic situational A when one has disturbed oneself about some aspect of that A. However, there may be times when direct modification of the situational A without prior belief change may yield effective results for the person even though that person has disturbed themselves about the critical A embedded in the situation. An example would be a client who, after making himself unhealthily angry, evicts a threatening lodger from his house. This person might have achieved similar results feeling healthily rather than unhealthily angry towards the lodger, but since his goal was to get rid of the lodger, his unhealthy anger did not interfere with him achieving his goal. This shows that while REBT therapists may have their preferences about the type of change that clients make and how they make them, it is not dogmatic in its views about such change.

When your client cannot or will not change A

The REBT version of the famous serenity prayer urges people to change the situational A when it can be changed with a minimum of self-created disturbance and to accept – but not like – it when we cannot change the situational A. Indeed, when A cannot be changed, your clients are thrown back to a stark choice: to disturb themselves about the unchanging A or not disturb themselves about this unchanging situation. To paraphrase Shakespeare: To disturb yourself or not to disturb yourself – that is the question. When this choice is made so explicit, clients most often go for the 'not disturb myself' option. When this happens, you can engage your client in the work of belief change. However, sometimes the client will not engage with you at the level of belief change and you may have to work at the level of inferential change, for example.

Although we have discussed the point that you may sometimes have to engage your client at the level of inferential change because they won't engage with you at the level of belief change, this is such an important point that a further example is necessary. Let us look at a case that my (WD) friend and colleague, Richard Wessler, related to me when he was an REBT therapist, and which I have quoted a number of times in my writings.

Dr Wessler's client was enraged every time her 90-year-old father telephoned her and enquired, 'Noo, what's doing?' As we can see (below) from the situationally-based ABC assessment that Dr Wessler conducted, what his client was most enraged about was her father's intrusion into her private life.

Situational A = My father telephones me and says, 'Noo, what's doing?'

Critical A = My father is intruding into my private life.

Irrational belief = My father must not intrude into my private life.

Emotional consequence = Unhealthy anger.

According to common REBT practice, Dr Wessler attempted to engage his client in belief change and challenged her rigid demand that her father must not intrude into her private life – but with no success. The client had tried to dissuade her father from being intrusive and even to begin a telephone conversation in a different way, but her father did not understand either of her points and kept beginning each phone call with his customary, 'Noo, what's doing?' The client was adamant that she did not want to discourage her father from phoning. He was an aged parent and she, being the only child, wanted regular telephone contact with her father. He just had to stop intruding into her private life.

So far, Dr Wessler has tried to engage his client in belief change work which she has resisted, and in changing the situational A by attempting to modify her father's behaviour and by refusing to take his phone calls. She was unsuccessful in the former strategy and unwilling to implement the latter strategy. In effect, she was facing a situational A that she couldn't or wouldn't change. In light of this Dr Wessler engaged his client in inferential change work which proved to be successful. He helped her to see that far from being intrusive into her private life, the greeting 'Noo, what's doing?' was his customary way of beginning a telephone conversation. She came to this conclusion after speaking with the other relatives that her father was accustomed to telephoning. They all confirmed that he began each call with his cheery 'Noo, what's doing?' greeting. She reinterpreted her critical A to 'My father is not intruding into my private life. His "Noo, what's doing?" greeting is his customary way of beginning telephone conversations.' Her new ABC, which reflects this change, is as follows:

Situational A = My father telephones me and says 'Noo, what's doing?'

Critical A = My father is not intruding into my private life. This is his customary way of beginning telephone conversations.

Irrational belief = None activated.

Unhealthy negative emotional consequence = None experienced.

As we pointed out earlier in this chapter, the problem with inferential change is that the person making the change retains her irrational belief. All she has achieved is to de-activate the irrational belief in the relevant situations. This means that if it transpires that the person goes back to her original critical A then she will once again activate her irrational belief with the consequence that she will disturb herself again. Thus, if Dr Wessler rethinks the client's new inference and concludes that she was right in the first place and that her father's greeting does indicate that he is intruding into her private life, she will activate her original irrational belief ('He must not intrude into my private life') and thereby make herself unhealthily angry again.

Behavioural Change

Behavioural change occurs when clients do not change their irrational beliefs, but improve by effecting constructive changes in their behaviour. Such constructive change occurs under two major conditions: i) when clients replace dysfunctional behaviour with constructive behaviour, and ii) when they acquire constructive patterns of behaviour, which have previously have been absent from their skill repertoire.

Of course, when clients change their behaviour for whatever reason, they can effect changes in belief. Indeed, as we will discuss later, acting on your newly developed rational beliefs is perhaps the best way of deepening your conviction in them. However, here we are concerned with instances where behaviour change does not promote belief change.

Helping clients by encouraging them to replace dysfunctional behaviour with constructive behaviour

Clients often have emotional problems partly because they do not use skills that are currently in their skills repertoire and are instead employing dysfunctional behavioural strategies. The REBT view of psychological disturbance is that even though clients may use dysfunctional behavioural strategies, they disturb themselves because they hold one or more irrational beliefs in relevant situations. Thus, the preferred REBT strategy is to help such clients deal first with their psychological disturbance by helping them to identify, challenge and change their disturbance-creating irrational beliefs and then to address their dysfunctional behaviour. However, some clients do not see or do not wish to see the sense of dealing with their irrational beliefs before tackling their dysfunctional behaviour. With such clients, REBT therapists need to be flexible and work at the behavioural level rather than the preferred belief level. For example, Hilary was a talented poet, but was scared of performing her poems in public. When she came to see me, I (WD) first endeavoured to get at the heart of her anxiety and discovered that she was most scared of freezing in front of her audience. She demanded that this must not happen and if it did she would conclude that she was defective as a person. I failed to help her change this irrational belief and think healthily about the possibility of freezing in public. So I changed tack and decided to assess her skills at reading her poetry aloud. I discovered that she was reading them too quickly, so I advised her to read them more slowly and to breathe more slowly during reading. She practised these simple modifications to her behaviour and gave a number of successful poetry readings. This led her to change her inference about the likelihood of freezing while reading her poetry. She now thought that with the skills I had taught her that it was highly unlikely that she would freeze, whereas before she had thought that it was quite likely that this would happen. However, even though she made changes at both the behavioural and inferential levels, she still thought irrationally about freezing in public. In other words, the changes that she made in her behaviour and in her inferences did not precipitate belief change.

Dealing with 'safety behaviours'

Clients often unwittingly perpetuate their psychological problems by the understandable but unhelpful use of so called 'safety behaviours'. From the perspective of the client, these behaviours keep them safe from threat and other actual or inferred aversive events, both external and internal. However, their enactment only serves to perpetuate the client's problems. This is the case for two main reasons: first, safety behaviours are carried out to help the client avoid facing certain events that are, from the client's frame of reference, highly aversive – examples being everyone laughing at the client and the client having a heart attack. Now these aversive events are in reality very low probability events, but are emotionally processed at the time as high probability events, although when the client calms down he can see that they are low probability events. From an REBT perspective, these events are cognitive consequences of prior irrational beliefs. Thus when the client engages in 'safety behaviour' he is actually reinforcing these prior irrational beliefs by acting to avoid their cognitive products.

Second, as the noted cognitive therapist Salkovskis (1996) has observed, when a client engages in 'safety behaviour' to ward off these highly aversive inferred events, they do not get the *experience* of learning that such events are unlikely to occur. I stress the word 'experience' here because cognitive learning is not sufficient; rather, the learning needs to be experiential if this point is to be truly grasped and integrated into the client's belief system. Unless this point is truly learned and acted on, the client will continue to enact 'safety behaviours' and thus keep himself falsely 'safe' in the short term , but perpetuate his problems in the longer term. For this reason, I (WD) call such 'safety behaviours' 'short-term safety-seeking behaviours with long-term unproductive results'.

In REBT, the best way to encourgae a client to deal productively with such behaviours is to:

1 help the client understand the nature of such 'safety-seeking behaviours', why the person engages in such behaviours and why they are ultimately self-defeating;
2 help the client develop alternative constructive behaviours and to see the differing effects of these behaviours, i.e. they enable the client to

practise appropriate rational beliefs and to test out the likelihood of the relevant aversive events occurring;

3   help the client to develop the appropriate rational beliefs;
4   encourage the client to rehearse the appropriate rational beliefs while engaging in the relevant constructive behaviours and resisting the urge to engage in the aforementioned safety-seeking behaviours;
5   process the outcomes of such homework assignments and repeat as necessary.

Teaching clients skills that are absent from their skills repertoire

The example of Hilary (pp. 25–6) is one of a client being helped by changing unconstructive behaviour to more constructive behaviour that was in her repertoire. But, as mentioned at the beginning of this section, sometimes clients can be helped at the behavioural level by learning skills that are absent from their behavioural skills repertoire. Thus, a client may be deficient in social skills, dating skills, assertion skills, study skills – to name but a few – and when they learn such skills they may bring about a favourable change in their environment, for example, others will respond to them more positively than before. The trouble with teaching clients skills in which they are deficient without helping them to change their irrational beliefs to rational beliefs, is that the activation of their irrational beliefs in real-life settings may well either inhibit clients from utilising their newly acquired skills altogether, or may interfere with the skilful execution of these skills. On the other hand, when clients change their irrational beliefs to rational beliefs, such change will not, on its own, help them acquire skills that are absent from their skills repertoire. Thus, in REBT, we prefer to help our clients over their psychological disturbance by helping them to change their irrational beliefs to rational beliefs, before helping them to acquire skills not present in their skills repertoire. As part of this skills-acquisition process, we also help our clients challenge and change irrational beliefs that may inhibit skills practice or interfere with the competent execution of these developing skills. If clients are unwilling or unable to change relevant irrational beliefs, we try to help them by encouraging them to change any distorted inferences at A, or by helping them to become so competent at their developing skills that their competence at these skills may distract them from their disturbance-creating irrational beliefs. Here, as elsewhere, REBT is a flexible approach to psychotherapy where preferred strategies give way to less preferred strategies to meet clients' therapeutic 'needs'.

Belief change

According to REBT theory, belief change is considered to be the type of change that best promotes the psychological health of the person. But what does this type of change involve? As we discussed in Chapter 1,

REBT posits that four irrational beliefs lie at the core of psychological disturbance, namely rigid demands, awfulising beliefs, low frustration tolerance beliefs and depreciation beliefs. The healthy, rational alternatives to these beliefs are: full preferences, non-awfulising beliefs, high frustration tolerance beliefs and acceptance beliefs.

Let us illustrate the content of belief change with a case example. Mary, a 24-year-old divorced woman was anxious about going on the dating scene again in case she was rejected by a man in whom she was interested. As a result of her anxiety, she avoided going to social gatherings. Putting this into the ABC framework, we have:

Situational A = Thinking about a man in whom I am interested.

Critical A = Being rejected by the man in whom I am interested.

B = I must not be rejected by the man in whom I am interested. If I am, then this would prove that I am unlovable.

C (emotional) = Anxiety.
C (behavioural) = Avoidance of social gatherings.
C (cognitive) = Predicting that such rejection is very likely.

Let us now imagine that Mary has achieved a belief change on this issue. How would this type of change affect her feelings, behaviour and subsequent thoughts at C?

Situational A = Thinking about a man in whom I am interested.

Critical A = Being rejected by the man in whom I am interested.

B = I don't want to be rejected by the man in whom I am interested, but there is no reason why this must not happen. If I this does happen, it does not mean that I am unlovable; it means that I am a fallible human being with whom some people are going to be interested in having a relationship and others are not.

C (emotional) = Concern.
C (behavioural) = Attending social gatherings.
C (cognitive) = Predicting that such rejection may happen, but that its likelihood is far less than when judged from an anxious frame of mind.

There are two important points to note from this example. First, the situational and critical A is the same in both scenarios. As we mentioned earlier, belief change is best facilitated when the critical A stays constant. If Mary changed this A as well as changing B, it is possible to argue that the change at B was predicated on the change at A and if A had not changed, the change at B would not have happened. If this was the case, then we could say that the belief change was not as robust as it would have been if A had not been changed.

Thus, let's suppose that Mary thought that the man in whom she was interested would also show interest in her (change in critical A), but that she now thought that if he did reject her she could still accept herself (change in B). Under these circumstances, we do not know whether Mary's change at B occurred only because she thought that she would be accepted by the man in whom she was interested and not rejected by him. The only way we can assess whether Mary's change at B is robust is to put her in a situation where she again predicts that she might be rejected by a man in whom she is interested. If she feels anxious about the impending rejection and avoids the man socially because she thinks that if she met him it is highly likely that he will reject her, then her belief change is not robust. However, if she feels concerned about being rejected, does not avoid the man socially and thinks that while rejection may occur there is also a chance that he may not reject her, then her belief change is robust.

The second point that we want you to note from Mary's example concerns the effect that her belief change has had on the consequences at C. You will note that changing her irrational belief to its rational alternative had a constructive impact on her emotions, her behaviour and her subsequent thinking. Emotionally, Mary became concerned about the prospect of being rejected by a man in whom she was interested, rather than anxious about it. Behaviourally, her belief change enabled her to attend social gatherings rather than avoid them. And cognitively, Mary's rational thinking at B led to thinking at C that was more realistic than it was when Mary held an irrational belief at B. What this example shows is that if someone changes their belief at B about a negative activating event at A, then it can have far-reaching consequences on their emotions, behaviour and subsequent thinking at C. The extent of the effects of belief change is not matched by the effects of the other changes that we have discussed (inferential change and behavioural change). Thus, let's suppose that Mary rethought her original inference at A and concluded that it was highly unlikely that she would be rejected by a man in whom she was interested. If she thought this then she would certainly not be anxious about being rejected or even concerned about this happening because she would view it as a low probability event. This would mean that she would go to social gatherings and if her subsequent thinking were unrealistic it would be unrealistically positive. But, Mary's irrational belief would still be intact and thus render her very vulnerable to emotional disturbance if she was actually rejected by a man in whom she was interested or if she thought that such rejection was likely.

Now, let's suppose that Mary made a behavioural change and went to social gatherings rather than avoiding them. As a result, she could conclude that being rejected by a man in whom she was interested was a low probability event and achieve the same gains as described above. However, she could just as easily conclude that being rejected by a man in whom she was interested was a high probability event, a negative critical A that would trigger her irrational belief. This, in turn, would lead her to feel anxious and prompt her to leave the situation and to think in a highly distorted manner. Thus, behaviour change without belief change renders the client's process of change unstable and unpredictable.

Belief change facilitates other types of change, but the opposite does not necessarily hold

We have made the point a number of times already in this book that changes at B are more robust and farther reaching than changes at A or than behavioural changes, and we will continue to stress this throughout the rest of the book. For this is one of the major cornerstones of the REBT perspective on psychotherapeutic change. One of the implications of this point is that once a client has made a belief change, he is in a better frame of mind to make related changes. Thus, changing one's irrational belief to its rational alternative helps a client adopt a healthy emotional response to the critical A and to stand back and take an objective viewpoint which will help him to reconsider the validity of his critical inference at A, and to change this if it proves to be distorted. Such objectivity is far less likely when the person is reconsidering his critical A while still holding an irrational belief. For example, Brian receives a note from his tutor to attend a meeting with the tutor and infers that the essay he has written is poor, and he disturbs himself about this critical A. If he temporarily assumes that his inference is true and changes his irrational belief to a rational belief, he is likely to consider that there were other, more valid reasons for his tutor's request than the poor quality of his essay. He would then be more able to choose one of these alternative inferences as the most probable in this situation than he would if he considered this issue while still holding his irrational belief. His irrational belief would lead to emotional disturbance and a biased frame of mind, conditions not conducive to an objective reconsideration of the validity of his critical inference.

In the same way that changing irrational beliefs to rational beliefs facilitates inferential change, it also facilitates behavioural change. It does so in two main ways. First, as we showed in Chapter 1, while irrational beliefs tend to lead to dysfunctional behaviour, rational beliefs tend to lead to more functional behaviour. Second, holding rational beliefs encourages the client to stand back and think about the way that he is behaving and to formulate more functional ways of acting. His rational beliefs will then help him to have the presence of mind to implement these new more constructive behaviours.

We have just shown how belief change can facilitate other types of change – in particular, inferential change and behavioural change. However, inferential change and behavioural change does not so readily lead to enduring belief change. Let's take inferential change first. You will recall that earlier in this chapter, we discussed the case of Mark who disturbed himself when he inferred that his lecturer ignored him at a local art gallery, because he held the following irrational belief: 'My lecturer absolutely should not have ignored me and it's terrible that he did. Poor me!' We have already made the point that were Mark to change this irrational belief and hold a rational belief instead, then he would be likely to stand back and question the validity of this inference and conclude that there were other more plausible explanations for his lecturer not seeing him at the gallery. However, if he re-evaluated his inference and concluded, for example, that his lecturer did not ignore him, but rather did not see him, then in all probability he would still cling to his irrational belief: 'My lecturer absolutely should not have ignored me and it's terrible that he did. Poor me!' His change of inference, therefore would not help him to change his underlying irrational belief. In order to do this he would have to assume, albeit temporarily, that his lecturer *did* ignore him, so that he could challenge his irrational belief while focusing on this critical A. This is why, in order to facilitate belief change in REBT, we encourage our clients to assume temporarily that their critical inferences are true.

Now let's consider behavioural change. Behavioural change can facilitate belief change, but it can easily be a stimulus for client self-disturbance or it may lead to inferential change without accompanying belief change. Behavioural change can lead to belief change when – as part of changing their behaviour – clients focus on their negative critical As and explicitly or implicitly change their irrational beliefs as a result. However, as already noted, this focus may lead clients to disturb themselves about the critical A because they rehearse their irrational beliefs.

Let us look at how this may operate in real life. Let's suppose that Jean does not assert herself with her boss because she is afraid he might disapprove of her. However, she attends an assertiveness training course that teaches her the skills of assertion, but does not help her to identify, challenge and change her assertion-inhibiting irrational belief: 'I must not be disapproved of by my boss and, if I am, it proves that I am worthless.' However, thanks to the skills practice that she did on the course, her confidence in her ability to assert herself has grown and she decides to assert herself with her boss. Several things can happen as a result of her decision:

1   Before asserting herself with her boss, Jean predicts that he will disapprove of her. She rehearses her irrational belief that he must not disapprove of her and that she is worthless if he does, and feels anxious as a result.
2   Before asserting herself with her boss, Jean predicts that he will disapprove of her. She realises that, while she would prefer this not to happen, it does not mean that it must not happen, and that if it does she is not worthless and can accept herself in the face of his disapproval. She feels concerned, but not anxious as a result.
3   Before asserting herself with her boss, Jean predicts that he will give her a fair hearing and will not disapprove of her.
4   After asserting herself with her boss, Jean concluded that he did disapprove of her. She rehearsed her irrational belief about this and became depressed.
5   After asserting herself with her boss, Jean concluded that he did disapprove of her. She realised that while she preferred this not to happen this did not mean that it absolutely should not have happened, and

just because it did, she is not worthless and can accept herself in the face of his disapproval. She felt sad about his disapproval, pleased that she had asserted herself and resolved to assert herself in the future whenever appropriate.

6   After asserting herself with her boss, Jean concluded that he gave her a fair hearing and did not disapprove of her.

This shows us that behaviour change (and the anticipation of such change) is the context for a) belief change in scenarios 2 and 5; b) disturbance in scenarios 1 and 4; and c) inferential change in scenarios 3 and 6. This demonstrates the unreliability of behaviour change for promoting belief change.

In summary, we have shown that belief change is quite a reliable facilitator of other types of change, namely inferential, behavioural and emotional change, but these others types of change are less reliable in promoting belief change.

In the field of change, REBT is perhaps best known for its position that meaningful and therapeutic emotional change is founded on belief change. Is the effect of emotional change on belief change as reliable? The answer is no. If we look at instances where a person's disturbed emotional state is altered by non-psychological means, as a result of drugs – either prescribed or non-prescribed – or by alcohol, it is unlikely that this emotional change will lead to the person changing his irrational beliefs to their rational equivalents. For example, Freda has been prescribed a tranquilliser to take when required. She tends to take this tranquilliser before going to a social function because she becomes anxious even thinking about attending such a function. Her anxiety is based on the irrational belief that she must be interesting, and that if she isn't, it proves that she is a boring person. The effects of the tranquilliser are that they calm her mood and she is able to get through the evening without too much bother. But has her drug-induced emotional change helped her to change her irrational belief? Let us see. If you were to ask Freda about her thinking during the evening, she would say, 'The drugs help me to focus away from thinking about how interesting I am being. If I think about the possibility of being boring, my thoughts are hazy and don't connect with my feelings. I'm in a kind of "who cares" frame of mind. At the end of the day I'm just glad to get the ordeal over, but I know that I have only done so because of the drugs. I'm dependent on them.' Does this seem as if the emotional change that Freda's drugs have brought about has occasioned a change in her irrational belief? It doesn't appear so. Even when in the situation in question, Freda appears to be in a detached, hazy frame of mind and can't connect with her preoccupation with being interesting. She certainly doesn't seem to hold a rational belief about being interesting, namely, 'I would like to be interesting, but I certainly don't need to be. If I'm not, I am not a boring person; rather, I am a fallible person who was uninteresting to certain people this evening.' If she held this belief,

Freda would experience healthy concern rather than hazy detachment. Freda's experience is widespread, for substance-induced emotional change rarely leads to belief change in the situation in which the emotional shift has been effected, and even more rarely does it lead to more enduring belief change.

The continuum of belief change

Irrational beliefs can range from being very specific to being highly general. The following are a number of irrational beliefs that vary along a specific–general continuum and are listed from specific to general:

- I must have the approval of my history teacher when I give him my essay.
- I must have the approval of all of my teachers when I give them my essays.
- I must have the approval of people in authority when they evaluate my work.
- I must have the approval of people in authority at all times.
- I must have the approval of all people who are significant to me.
- I must have the approval of everyone.

Specific irrational beliefs can be specific examples of more general irrational beliefs (as above) or they can exist in their own right and not be related to general beliefs. Quite naturally, it is easier to change specific irrational beliefs than more general ones, particularly when these specific beliefs are not related to general irrational beliefs. Specific irrational beliefs are more narrow in scope and occupy a less central position in the person's belief system, particularly if they are not related to general irrational beliefs. They lead to a smaller number of dysfunctional behaviours and the person employs fewer defensive procedures. By contrast, general irrational beliefs are broader in scope and occupy a more central position in the client's belief system. They lead to a larger number of dysfunctional behaviours and a greater number of distorted subsequent inferences, and the client who has them employs a greater number of defensive procedures.

Normally, clients change specific irrational beliefs before they change general irrational beliefs, but there are times when clients first change general irrational beliefs and then change the specific irrational beliefs which stem from these general beliefs. When the latter occurs, the person is able to deal with more abstract concepts and can move from the abstract level of cognition to the specific level of cognition quite easily.

The interdependence principle of change

So far in this chapter, we have considered the different types of change as separate from one another. In reality, however, they do overlap and influence one another. This mirrors the point that we made in Chapter 1 that the ABCs interact with one another and cannot, in reality, be treated separately from one another. However, as we have shown in this chapter the impact of belief change on other forms of change is more widespread and enduring than the impact of these other forms of change on one another and on belief change. But, as we will discuss later, one can only truly achieve belief change if one acts and thinks in ways that are consistent with the rational beliefs that one is attempting to acquire and usually only if one is prepared to do so repeatedly over time. This briefly demonstrates the complex relationships that exist among As, Bs and Cs and among the different types of change discussed in this chapter. It is beyond the scope of this book to discuss these complex relationships fully, but we will discuss some of these relationships when they become relevant.

In the next chapter, we will outline REBT's perspective on the steps that clients need to take in order to achieve psychotherapeutic change.

In this chapter, we will focus on belief change in the therapeutic setting and outline the steps that clients need to take if they are to achieve belief change. We will consider specific belief change here, and in the final chapter we will discuss how such change can be generalised and address the concept of general belief change. Let us be clear at the outset we are not saying the following steps need to be taken in the precise order that we outline them, nor are we saying that all the steps need to be taken for change to occur. Rather, following the steps is important, and for most clients, under most conditions, taking them all will increase the likelihood that specific belief change will occur.

1 The client accepts that he has a problem that he wants to change

It may seem obvious that your client has to admit to a problem before he does anything to change it, but it is a step that a number of counsellors assume that their clients have taken, without checking to see whether this is the case. This is particularly true for novice REBT therapists. Such therapists hear their clients disclose an unhealthy negative emotion and automatically think that because REBT theory states that the disclosed negative emotion is unhealthy, their client is bound to want to change it. While this is often the case, it is not invariably so, and it is usually worth spending time discussing with your clients how they view their unhealthy negative emotions and whether or not they wish to change them. In our clinical experience, clients are particularly likely to be ambivalent about changing guilt and unhealthy anger. DiGiuseppe (1988) has written a very interesting article on this point. He argues that we have ideas about what emotions we are supposed to feel in given situations, and even though these emotions may be painful to us and we are willing to see them as problematic, if we regard them as inevitable parts of specific episodes, then we may not think that they can be changed. Unless you explore such issues with your clients you may encounter client resistance later in the change process.

2   Your client accepts psychological responsibility for his problem

Your client may readily acknowledge that his unhealthy negative emotion is a problem for him and may well wish to change this feeling, but if he does not take psychological responsibility for the problem then he will look to change the situational A rather than to change B as a solution to the problem. Assuming psychological responsibility for his problem involves your client accepting that while the situation at A may contribute to his emotional problem at C, it does not cause it. Rather, your client appreciates that it is something that he thinks that largely determines his reaction at C. This is why I (WD) make such a fuss when my trainees use 'A "causes" C' language in their work with clients (such as 'How did it make you feel?' instead of the preferred 'How did you feel about it?').

3   Your client understands the critical role that the specific irrational belief plays in determining his problem

Elsewhere, I (WD) have distinguished between two types of psychological responsibility: general and specific (Dryden, 1995). General psychological responsibility is what Epictetus was referring to in his famous dictum: 'Men are disturbed not by things, but by their views of things.' It is this type of psychological responsibility that we referred to in the previous point. However, in order to change a specific irrational belief, your client has to acknowledge the crucial role that it plays in determining his emotional, behavioural and cognitive consequences at C in the ABC model. This is what is meant by specific psychological responsibility. It can be summed up in a modification of Epictetus' dictum: 'Men are disturbed not by things, but by the irrational beliefs that they hold about things.'

4   Your client identifies realistic goals for change

When your client has identified a problematic emotion (and/or a dys-functional behaviour), in order to give a direction to the change process it is important that you help your client set goals that he can work towards. It is important that these goals be realistic and in the context of the ongoing existence, at least temporarily, of the negative activating event at A. This latter point is an important part of the process of belief change. For example, one of my (WD) clients was anxious about being rejected by a woman if he asked her to dance. His ABC was:

> Situational A = At a dance thinking about asking a woman to dance.
> Critical A = The possibility of being rejected by the woman.
> B = I must not be rejected and if I am it proves that I am worthless.

C (emotional) = Anxiety.
C (behavioural) = Going to dances, but not asking women to dance.
C (cognitive) = The vast majority of women will refuse to dance with me.

Now, in order to achieve belief change, this client has to confront being rejected so that he can practise thinking rationally in the face of this situation. As we discussed at the end of the previous chapter, this is why in REBT we prefer not to help clients change A before B, because doing so reduces their interest in changing B, leaving them vulnerable to future disturbance should A recur.

So, in order for this client to change his belief, he has to contemplate his critical A occurring, i.e. he has to consider being rejected by a woman and to work through the experience so that cognitively he arrives at the following:

Situational A = At a dance thinking about asking a woman to dance.

Critical A = The possibility of being rejected by the woman.

B = I would prefer not to be rejected, but there is no reason why I must not be rejected. If I am, it does not prove that I am worthless. It proves that I am the same fallible human being as I would be if I was accepted.

C (emotional) = Concern

C (behavioural = Going to dances and taking the risk of asking women to dance

C (cognitive) = Some women will women refuse to dance with me, but others will dance with me

This new ABC formulation provides this client with his realistic goals: emotional, behavioural and cognitive. Let's look at each of these goals in turn.

Emotional goal

Instead of being anxious about asking a woman to dance and risking the possibility of being turned down, the client has stated that his goal is to be concerned, but not anxious about this happening. This is a good example of a client choosing a healthy negative emotion as a goal instead of an unhealthy negative emotion.

This is an important point. Many clients, when asked what their emotional goal is when facing a negative activating event, reply that they want to feel less anxious or that they want to feel relaxed. In REBT, we argue that both of these goals are problematic. Achieving the first goal can only be done either by changing A or by reducing the strength of one's conviction in one's irrational belief. The second goal is problematic because for it to be achieved the person has to convince himself that he doesn't care about something which he does, in reality, care about.

Behavioural goal

Instead of going to dances and standing on the sidelines, the client sets as a goal going to dances and taking the risk of asking women to dance. We mentioned earlier that behavioural consequences of holding beliefs at B involve either actual behaviours or action tendencies (sometimes known as behavioural impulses or urges to act). It is important that you help your client set as his behavioural goal actions that are consistent with his rational belief. Having this behavioural goal clearly in mind will help him to resist acting on his action tendencies that are associated with his problem emotion which he will still tend to experience until he has made sufficient progress at changing his irrational belief.

Cognitive goal

As we noted earlier in this book, the beliefs that you hold have an impact on your subsequent thinking at C. The latter type of thinking is known as cognitive consequences. The client, in our example, realised that when he was anxious his subsequent thinking was distorted and unrealistic (i.e. 'The vast majority of women will refuse to dance with me'). So he set as a cognitive goal something more realistic and undistorted (i.e. 'Some women will women refuse to dance with me, but others will dance with me').

   While people are less likely to specify cognitive goals than they are emotional and behavioural goals, it is our view that helping clients to set cognitive goals aids the change process in that it ensures that emotional, behavioural and cognitive goals are lined up in a coherent and consistent way. It is this consistency and coherence that helps to facilitate psycho-therapeutic change.

5   Your client commits himself to achieving these goals

It is one thing to identify realistic goals for change, but another thing to commit oneself to achieve these goals. Making such a commitment involves your client investing time and energy in following a plan designed to achieve these goals. It involves him accepting responsibility for initiating and maintaining the change-related activities that are designed to lead to goal achievement. This means he must practise the many cognitive, imagi-nal, emotive and behavioural methods that are part of the technical side of REBT. In some cases, it facilitates the psychotherapeutic change process for your client to make a public commitment to achieve his goals, while in other cases such public commitment may not aid the change process and doing so may occasionally impede client goal achievement.

Some clients do better in implementing their commitment if they are involved with other people who have made a similar commitment, while others prefer to work on their own and would be put off were they to work in concert with like-minded individuals implementing similar commitments. The important ingredient here seems to be some form of commitment made in accord with the individual's commitment- related preferences.

6 Your client recognises that the key to achieving his goals is changing his target specific irrational belief

It will have become apparent by now that beliefs are mediating variables, i.e. they mediate between events and emotional, behavioural and cognitive responses to these events. When these responses are unhealthy, the beliefs that mediate between these responses and the relevant events are irrational and when they are healthy the mediating beliefs are rational. We have made these points to emphasise that when your client has an emotional problem, he does not set thinking rationally as his goal. Rather, as we showed you in point 4 above, he is likely to select an emotion and/or a behaviour as a goal and see rational thinking as a means to achieve this goal. So the key to this particular step is that your client fully acknowledges that, in order to achieve the realistic goals he has set for himself, it is important to change the irrational beliefs that mediate his unhealthy responses. Without this understanding, he will not direct himself to his specific irrational belief as a precursor to change.

7 Your client sees that the specific rational belief is a plausible, believable alternative to his specific irrational belief and will facilitate goal achievement

Having accepted that he needs to change his specific irrational belief in order to achieve his goals, the next step is for your client to construct an alternative to this belief that is plausible and believable. If he does not see this alternative belief as plausible, he will not be inclined to commit himself to acquire and truly believe it. In addition, he also has to accept that while he does not have a strong conviction in this rational belief, it is something that he can see himself believing at some point in the future, i.e. he finds the new rational alternative belief believable. Finally, although in the previous step your client acknowledged that changing his irrational belief was a key step in achieving his goals, this is not the same as seeing clearly that acquiring this particular specific rational belief will lead to goal achievement.

8   Your client understands intellectually that his specific irrational belief is unhelpful, inconsistent with reality and illogical while the alternative rational belief is helpful, consistent with reality and logical

One of the key tasks that therapists and clients have always had in REBT, from its very inception, is to dispute or question the latter's irrational beliefs. DiGiuseppe (1991) has written a seminal paper on cognitive disputing which repays careful study. In that paper, DiGiuseppe makes the point that it is also important for therapists and clients to dispute or question the latter's rational beliefs. The initial purpose of this questioning is to help clients clearly see that their specific irrational beliefs are unhelpful, false and illogical and their alternative specific rational beliefs are, by contrast, helpful, true and logical. At this point, REBT therapists only expect their clients to achieve what has been called 'intellectual insight' into these points. They do not expect them to truly believe it yet. In an early paper, Albert Ellis (1963) defined intellectual insight as a lightly and occasionally held conviction in something which does not influence one's feelings and behaviour in significant ways.

'Intellectual insight' is not, therefore, the end goal of the disputing process. Rather, it is a beginning goal of this process. When clients indicate that they have intellectual insight (but not emotional insight) into the points under consideration, they say things like: 'I understand that believing that I must have my parent's approval isn't true, sensible or useful, but I only see that in my head. In my heart I still really believe that I need their approval' or, more generally, 'I understand it intellectually, but I don't feel it emotionally', and 'I see it up here [pointing to one's head], but I don't feel it in here [pointing to one's gut].'

9   Your client understands that intellectual insight is important but insufficient for belief change

Here, it is important that you explain to your client that intellectual insight is a natural stage in the belief change process and that without it your client wouldn't understand why his specific irrational belief is unhelpful, false and illogical and why his rational belief is helpful, true and logical and would therefore not see the point of belief change. There is another reason why intellectual insight is important: it gives your client an opportunity to reflect on all the arguments about the two competing beliefs and make an informed decision whether or not he really wants to change the specific irrational belief in favour of its rational alternative. Thus, we suggest that you encourage your clients to see the value of so-called intellectual insight and not to disparage it. If it wasn't for intellectual insight, your client might end up truly believing something that on reflection he would prefer not to believe.

Having said this, it is important that when your client seeks belief change he understands that since intellectual insight does not influence his feelings and behaviour, it is insufficient to promote significant belief change and so will not help him overcome his problem and achieve his goals.

10   Your client understands that emotional insight is required for belief change to be achieved

A moment ago we said that intellectual insight represents a lightly and occasionally held conviction in something which does not influence one's feelings and behaviour in significant ways. Ellis (1963) considers that emotional insight represents a strongly and frequently held conviction in something which does influence one's feelings and behaviour in significant ways. REBT's view of belief change, then, involves your client moving from intellectual insight to emotional insight, a process that we will discuss in a moment. But first it is worth mentioning that REBT has, at present, a quantitative model of belief change where intellectual insight and emotional insight are seen as existing on one continuum. This contrasts markedly with Teasdale and Barnard's (1993) model of interactive cognitive systems (known as the ICS model), which views these two forms of insight as qualitatively different and presumably, therefore, as existing along two continua. Teasdale (1996) has argued that there are ways of facilitating movement from one form of insight to the other, but is not at all clear in suggesting steps for how this can be done.

Two of the hallmarks of REBT theory are its flexibility and its permeability. As such, if it appears that intellectual insight and emotional insight are qualitatively rather than quantitatively different and this formulation yields clear guidelines for facilitating emotional insight, then REBT theory will be revised accordingly.

11   Your client understands that in order to achieve emotional insight, a number of steps have to be followed

As we have just mentioned, REBT theory considers that emotional insight exists along the same continuum as intellectual insight. It also outlines a number of steps that people can use to move from intellectual to emotional insight into their specific rational beliefs. Elsewhere, I (WD) have termed this process strengthening one's conviction in one's rational beliefs (Dryden, 1999) and there are a number of ways of facilitating this strengthening process.

Repetition

The first way for your client to strengthen conviction in his rational beliefs involves repetition: repetition of the disputing process. More specifically, it entails repeated questioning of specific irrational and rational beliefs. REBT has devised a number of self-help forms to aid this process. After developing and refining his skill at these forms, your client begins to do this for himself in his own head and the more he repeats the disputing process, the more he strengthens his conviction in his new rational belief.

Developing a rational portfolio

The second way to strengthen conviction in rational beliefs involves your client collecting a substantial body of arguments in favour of his target rational belief and against his target irrational belief, in the same way as a lawyer collects and collates information in favour of the proposition that his client is innocent and against the proposition that his client is guilty. Similarly, when your client can clearly see (albeit intellectually) that his specific irrational belief is unhelpful, false and illogical and that his specific rational belief is helpful, true and sensible, then he can commit himself to a process of collecting and collating a large body of information to this effect. I (WD) have devised a technique that formalises this process that I call the rational portfolio technique (Dryden, 1999). Of course, in helping your client to develop a rational portfolio of arguments, it is important that you do not imply that there are *no* unhelpful consequences of your client's specific irrational belief and that there are *no* helpful effects of his alternative specific rational belief. However, the flexible development of a portfolio of ideas concerning the irrationality of irrational beliefs and the rationality of rational beliefs does seem to help your client to strengthen his conviction in the specific rational belief under consideration and to weaken his conviction in his related irrational belief.

Rational judo

The third way to strengthen conviction in rational beliefs involves the principle of strengthening through developing responses to attack, a kind of rational judo, so to speak. After developing his alternative rational belief, your client can be encouraged to engage in a process of attacking this belief and responding to these attacks (see Dryden, 2001 for a description of one of these techniques known as the zig-zig technique) until he cannot develop any more attacks.

Mental rehearsal of rational beliefs

The fourth way to strengthen conviction in rational beliefs involves your client mentally rehearsing them (see Dryden, 1999 for a description of two such methods). Here, your client is encouraged to imagine the negative activating event about which he disturbed himself and to get in touch with his feelings and/or specific irrational belief about this event. Then, while he still imagines this same event, you encourage your client to change his feelings (by implicitly changing his specific irrational belief to its rational alternative) or to change his specific irrational belief explicitly (thereby gaining practice at changing his feelings).

Force and energy

The fifth way to strengthen conviction in rational beliefs involves the use of force and energy while employing specific techniques. Ellis (1994) has argued that the change process needs to be implemented forcefully and energetically by clients if they are to gain emotional insight into their rational beliefs. I (WD) have written on vivid methods in REBT (Dryden, 1986) where I argue that it is important for therapists to make REBT an emotional experience for clients rather than just an intellectual exercise, if meaningful belief change is to occur.

Belief–action–thinking consistency

The sixth way to strengthen conviction in rational beliefs calls upon your client to act and think in ways that are consistent with his specific rational belief and inconsistent with his specific irrational belief and to do this repeatedly. In particular, this involves your client dropping his behavioural and cognitive safety-seeking and overcompensation manoeuvres while simultaneously rehearsing his rational beliefs and acting and thinking constructively.

Persistence until feelings change

The seventh way to strengthen conviction in rational beliefs involves your client persisting with this process until his feelings change, using a variety of cognitive, imaginal and emotive techniques. We usually explain to clients that their feelings are likely to change well after they change their beliefs and their behaviour. It follows that your client needs to continue to practise thinking rationally and acting constructively until his feelings have begun to change. Unless your client acknowledges this, he may give up using the techniques of REBT because his feelings have not changed as quickly as he was expecting.

12   Your client recognises the non-linear process of psychotherapeutic change

Psychotherapeutic change is rarely a linear process. Sometimes your client will make great strides forward, sometimes he will make modest gains, while at other times he may not make any strides forward at all despite continuing to practise helpful belief–change-oriented techniques. Indeed, your client may even revert temporarily to old ways of irrational thinking for no easily discernible reason. Unless your client fully accepts the non-linear nature of psychotherapeutic change then, once again, he may well get discouraged, stop practising REBT techniques and revert once more to holding well-established irrational beliefs, this time less temporarily. However, if your client accepts this grim aspect of reality, he will continue to use REBT methods because he understands the process of psychotherapeutic change and knows that this slowing down, or even reversal, of change is part of the change process. Consequently, he will soon experience a quickening of this process.

13   Your client works to prevent relapse

It follows from what we have written above that your client will experience lapses in the psychotherapeutic change process and, if he is not careful, he may even experience a relapse. In our view, a lapse is a non-serious, usually brief, partial return to a problematic state, whereas a relapse is a serious, extended, full return to that state. In the drug and alcohol addiction field, the concept of relapse prevention is quite a common one and Ludgate (1995) has argued that it can be used profitably in cognitive-behavioural approaches to psychotherapy.

Working to prevent relapse basically involves your client i) dealing effectively with lapses so that they don't lead to a relapse; ii) learning to identify his vulnerabilities and dealing with them effectively so that they don't lead to lapses; and iii) identifying and dealing with idiosyncratic obstacles to change, a subject which we will presently discuss at some length.

14   Your client makes a lifetime commitment to psychotherapeutic change and resolves to act on this commitment

If you were to say to someone that once he has become physically fit he would not have to exercise again for the rest of his life in order to maintain such fitness, the person would laugh at you because he would rightly regard the idea to be preposterous. If asked to expand on this he would likely say that physical well-being has to be maintained and the only way to maintain it over one's lifetime is to make a lifetime commitment to exercise and to act on this commitment. However, if you told your client that when he had overcome his problem and had achieved a measure of psychological well-being he would need to work to maintain and enhance this level of psychological well-being, he would probably either balk at the idea or accept it, but not act on it.

However, if clients are to maintain and enhance their psychological gains, they will, in all probability, have to commit themselves to a programme of psychological exercise for the rest of their lives. We often say to our clients that they routinely devote well over an hour a day to activities that maintain their physical well-being (washing, eating, exercising, etc.) and would object if anyone suggested that they should not do this. We go on to say that if they were to devote about 30 minutes to their psychological well-being, every day, then they would go a long way to maintaining and enhancing this desirable state.

Finally, it is important that your client understands his role in initiating and maintaining the process of psychotherapeutic change. To this end, we encourage our clients to write down the following statement and to carry it around with them as they go about their daily business:

'The more steps I take, the more changes I will make.'

In the next chapter, we consider the role of the therapist in promoting psychotherapeutic change in REBT.

In this chapter, we will focus more specifically on the role of the therapist in promoting psychotherapeutic change in REBT. Our view in REBT is that both therapist and client have roles and responsibilities in the therapeutic process. As a therapist you are responsible for carrying out your role and responsibilities, and your client is responsible for carrying out his role and responsibilities once he knows about them and agrees to assume them. It follows that you are not responsible for your client carrying out his role and responsibilities, although you are responsible for those interventions which might increase the chances that he will implement his role and responsibilities, and you are also responsible for initiating and sustaining a dialogue concerning why your client is not carrying out the tasks for which he is responsible. It also follows that your client is not responsible for you carrying out your role and responsibilities. In this chapter, we will discuss your role as therapist in promoting psychotherapeutic change and in the next chapter we will discuss your client's role in promoting such change.

It goes without saying that as a therapist you have a very important bearing on whether or not your client achieves psychotherapeutic change and how much he changes during the process of REBT and after it has ended. You cannot realistically take full responsibility for client change for as we have just noted your client has his own responsibility here. But you do have an important role to play in the change process and in this chapter we will discuss this role and how you can best implement it.

The working relationship in REBT

All approaches to counselling and psychotherapy involve the therapist and client in a working relationship with one another. While we, in REBT, do not consider this relationship to be the sine qua non of psychotherapeutic change, we do think that it is an important vehicle for change, and any analysis of psychotherapeutic change in REBT which did not consider this working relationship would be sadly lacking.

The therapy relationship as relationship

If we break down the phrase 'working relationship' into its constituent parts we have the terms 'working' and 'relationship'. Although you and your client have a job of work to do in REBT, the relationship that you develop and maintain with your client has a decided impact on the work that you have come together to do. Ed Bordin (1979) has referred to the bond domain of the therapeutic alliance and this domain encompasses several relationship factors that have an impact on psychotherapeutic change. In this section we will discuss these factors from the standpoint of the therapist as the agent of such change, and will of course do so from an REBT perspective.

Core conditions

In a seminal paper, Carl Rogers (1957) argued that constructive therapeutic change followed when the client experienced the therapist as empathic, non-possessively warm and congruent in the therapeutic relationship and that these experienced conditions, which came be known as the 'core con-ditions', were necessary and sufficient for such change to occur. Ellis (1959) argued that while such conditions may well be important in help-ing promote client change in psychotherapy, they were neither necessary nor sufficient for clients to change. The current REBT views on each of the core conditions are listed below.

1 It is important that REBT therapists offer philosophic as well as affective empathy

When an REBT therapist communicates to her client that she understands how he feels from his frame of reference, this affective empathy strength-ens the client's bond to the therapist. However, REBT therapists also com-municate what is known as philosophic empathy: an empathic understanding of the clients' beliefs that underlie how they feel. This strengthens the client's bond to the therapist, but it also enables the ther-apist to set the scene for later disputing of the client's irrational beliefs.

2 It is important that REBT therapists unconditionally accept their clients

As we discussed earlier, the concept of unconditional acceptance as applied to humans incorporates the following ideas:

- Humans cannot legitimately be given a global rating.
- Humans are complex organisms comprising many positive, negative and neutral features.
- Humans are ever-changing organisms.
- Humans are fallible.
- All humans have equal worth by dint of being human.
- Humans differ markedly with respect to their behaviour and traits but not, as noted above, with respect to their work.

When the REBT therapist conveys to her client that she unconditionally accepts him, she displays some or preferably all of the above attitudes towards him, thus helping him to see that he can adopt the same philosophy of unconditional self-acceptance (USA). This does not mean that the therapist likes everything about the client. Far from it! However, skilled REBT therapists can help clients address their disagreeable behaviour while accepting them unconditionally.

3-It is important that REBT therapists are genuine and congruent in the therapeutic relationship

There are a number of dimensions of the core condition of genuineness/congruence that are relevant to the practice of REBT:

- The therapist often, but not always, expresses what she experiences – because REBT has relationship and technical features, an REBT therapist will express what she experiences to a) address problems in the therapeutic relationship, b) give the client valuable feedback about the way he may come across to people in everyday life, and c) to facilitate the technical side of REBT. The exception to such expression is when the therapist deems it likely that the client will unduly disturb himself about what the therapist expresses to him.
- The therapist engages in self-disclosure – at times, the REBT therapist will disclose to the client salient aspects about her own life. Normally, this disclosure will have educational value for the client and show the client a) that the therapist is human and has had similar problems to the client, and b) how the therapist successfully addressed these problems using REBT. This is known as the coping model of self-disclosure. However, the therapist will not self-disclose indiscriminately and will withhold such disclosure if she considers that the client will find it anti-therapeutic or will disturb himself about the disclosure.
- The therapist regularly uses REBT to address her own problems – this is an important but little considered subject in the REBT literature. My view (WD) is that the more effective REBT therapists regularly use REBT in their own lives and thus can talk more congruently about its use with their clients. By contrast, REBT therapists who do not use REBT in their own lives come across as wooden, theoretically based practitioners who do not embody the theory of REBT.

Therapeutic role

All approaches to counselling and psychotherapy conceive of the therapist's basic role in a certain way. For example, in existential therapy the therapist is seen as a guide accompanying the client on an existential journey, and in cognitive therapy the therapist adopts a role based on the principle of collaborati47ve empiricism. In REBT, the therapist seeks to collaborate with the client in a directed examination of the empirical and logical validity and pragmatic value of the client's dysfunctional thoughts and core (unhealthy) schemata.

In REBT, we regard the principle of collaborative empiricism as problematic in two respects. Firstly, while the client knows more about his experience than the therapist does, the therapist knows more about the professional constructs of the therapeutic approach than the client, and thus to expect them to collaborate as equals on this latter point is disingenuous. Secondly, while REBT therapists agree with their cognitive therapy colleagues that the empirical and pragmatic status of their clients' thoughts and schemata are important, we would also focus on the logical status of such cognitions, whereas this focus is not emphasized in cognitive therapy.

What, then, is the role that REBT therapists prefer to adopt in the conduct of this approach to psychotherapy? I (WD) call this role that of the authoritative, encouraging educator, which is rooted in realistic egalitarianism. Let us consider the different elements of this role.

1-Authoritative

REBT therapists are authoritative in the sense of being open about their expertise about REBT theory and practice and by communicating REBT concepts in a clear manner and with authority. This certainly does not mean that REBT therapists are authoritarian in that they brook no disagreement from clients about REBT concepts. Indeed, as we have made clear elsewhere, competent REBT therapists encourage their clients to identify and disclose their doubts, reservations and objections to REBT concepts and engage their clients in a respectful dialogue about these reservations. In doing so, REBT therapists do correct their clients' misconceptions about these concepts and do so with respect, but with authority.

2-Encouragement

REBT therapists encourage their clients in a number of ways:

- Encouragement for task completion – assuming that the therapist has correctly ascertained that the client does have the skills to perform a task, the therapist helps the client to see that if he applies himself then he will, in all probability, be able to complete the task. This holds whether the task is an REBT skill or something that the client has agreed to do for homework. In short, when encouraging the client in this domain, the therapist conveys a non-Pollyanna-ish 'You can do it' attitude to the client.
- Encouragement for goal attainment – here, the REBT therapist shows the client that if he persists in carrying out agreed homework assignments, he will increase the chances of achieving his goals. When encouraging the client in this domain, the therapist conveys a non-Pollyanna-ish 'You can achieve it' attitude to the client.

- Encouragement for dealing with lapses – at some point in the therapeutic process, clients will experience a lapse which we define as a partial and temporary return to a problem state. One of the major tasks that REBT therapists have is to prepare clients to deal effectively with such lapses when they occur. We will discuss this issue more fully later. However, once they have adequately prepared clients in this regard, then it is useful if REBT therapists encourage their clients by helping them to see that they can deal with lapses if they apply what they have been taught. Thus, when encouraging the client in this domain, the therapist conveys a non-Pollyanna-ish 'You can deal with lapses' attitude to the client.

3 Psychological educator

While REBT is a major approach to counselling and psychotherapy, it can also be seen as a leading approach to psychological education in that REBT therapists do need to teach their clients a number of principles, of which the following are notable examples:

- Much psychological disturbance is underpinned by irrational beliefs.
- A major step in the change process is for the client to identify and challenge his irrational beliefs.
- The best way for the client to gain conviction in his rational beliefs is for him to act and think in ways that are consistent with these new rational beliefs, and in ways that are inconsistent with the old irrational beliefs.

While REBT theory is clear concerning which principles REBT therapists need to teach their clients, it gives its practitioners a great deal of latitude with respect to how these principles are to be taught. Examples of creative methods of teaching rational principles can be found in Bernard & Wolfe (2000).

In teaching clients the principles of REBT, its practitioners are explicit about the fact that they are outlining but one approach to understanding emotional problems and their amelioration and not *the* approach to such matters. Therapeutic humility is an ethical approach to psychological education, in our view.

4 Realistic egalitarianism

We mentioned earlier REBT's reservations about the concept of 'collaborative empiricism'. REBT practice is rooted instead in what I (WD) call the principle of realistic egalitarianism in the therapeutic relationship. This principle has the following features:

- The therapist and client are equal in humanity. They are equal in worth as people, but unequal in certain respects. Thus, in some areas, the client may have better traits and greater talents than the therapist and in other areas the reverse may be the case.

- The client knows more than the therapist about his life and what he is disturbing himself about.
- The therapist knows more than the client about the theory and practice of REBT. In particular, she knows more than the client about psychological disturbance, its conceptualisation, perpetuation and amelioration from an REBT perspective.
- In working with the client, the REBT therapist acknowledges to herself and to her client where she considers them to be equals, and where she considers that they are not equals. The latter is done with tact and honesty. Ellis (in Dryden, 1990) has written an important article on this issue which repays close reading.

Therapeutic style

REBT is known as an active–directive approach to psychotherapy in that therapists are active in the encounter and direct their clients' attention to how to use REBT to help themselves address their problems effectively. The REBT therapist usually takes the lead in initiating and maintaining this structured approach to emotional problem-solving, although wherever possible – and especially towards the end of therapy – the therapist encourages the client to take the lead in structuring the process himself using the ABCDE framework (where 'D' stands for disputing irrational beliefs and 'E' for executing techniques to increase conviction in rational beliefs).

Having made the point that REBT therapists use an active–directive therapeutic style, here, as elsewhere, REBT therapists are flexible in that they vary their style according to their client. They are in Arnold Lazarus' (1989) words, 'an authentic chameleon, changing style, but doing so with authenticity'. The following will give you a flavour of the styles which REBT therapists adopt with their clients:

- humorous
- serious
- formal
- businesslike
- informal
- encouraging
- less active–directive (particularly with reactant clients)
- educational (here it is important to note that there are different teaching styles and effective REBT therapists are able to employ a variety of these styles)
- prompting (particularly in the later stages of therapy)

- self-disclosing
- non self-disclosing

In addition, REBT therapists vary their pace of interventions, working at a faster pace with those who think and process information quickly and at a slower pace with those who require more time to process information.

Communicator credibility

The final dimension of the therapeutic bond that we will consider concerns the credibility of the REBT therapist as a communicator. You will now be familiar with the idea that a major part of the REBT therapist's role is to communicate relevant rational principles which the client can use to overcome his problems and live a more fulfilled life. It is a well-established finding in the field of social psychology that people are not just influenced by the content of a message. Rather, they are more likely to pay attention to that message, digest it and be influenced by it if they find the communicator of that message credible. There are two major sources of communicator credibility that REBT therapists need to consider. These are the perceived expertness of the communicator and how likeable the communicator is.

Some clients will only listen to and be influenced by what you say if they perceive you to have the status of an expert. They may like you, but this is not the important factor for such people. Indeed, they may not like you and still be influenced by you if they think that you have the authority of an expert.

Other clients will only listen to you and be influenced by what you have to say if they like you. For such people, it doesn't matter that you are only starting out in your career as an REBT therapist. If they like you, then you may be able to influence them. If they don't like you then they won't listen to you, even if you are an expert in the field of REBT. On one of my (WD) regular trips to the Albert Ellis Institute, I was sitting in the lobby of the Institute when a woman, a new client of Dr Ellis, sat down next to me and told me angrily that she wasn't going to listen to anything Albert Ellis said because he wasn't nice to her and she didn't like him.

The therapy relationship as work

As we noted above, if the 'working relationship' is broken into constituent parts, we have the terms 'working' and 'relationship'. We dealt with the 'relationship' aspect of the working relationship above. In this section, we will look at the 'working' aspect of this relationship. As the term 'working' makes clear, you and your client have come together to work. You haven't come together to socialise or to get to know one another better romantically or sexually (although sadly this does happen when something goes drastically wrong in this *'working* relationship'); rather, you have come together to do a job of work: to help your client overcome his psychological problems and live more resourcefully. In his reconceptualisation of the old psychoanalytic term 'working alliance', Ed Bordin (1979) has pointed out that there are two working domains in the therapeutic relationship between therapist and client: the goal domain and the task domain (the third domain of this relationship is the bond domain which we discussed above).

The goal domain

In the goal domain, it is important that therapist and client have a clearly shared understanding about the client's goals. Problems in the working relationship can occur where the therapist thinks that the client's goal is 'X' when in fact it is 'Y'. This may occur because the therapist has not bothered to check with the client about the latter's goals or it may occur because the client has verbally stated that 'X' is his goal when his real, hidden goal is 'Y'. It follows from this that if your client's behaviour with respect to his stated goals is at variance with his words then it is important to explore the nature of this discrepancy (see Chapter 6).

As an REBT therapist it is important that you spend time discussing and negotiating your client's goals with him. In particular, you are advised not to assume that your client wishes to set as his emotional goal a healthy negative emotion in response to a negative activating event (for example, concern in response to threat when his unhealthy negative emotion is anxiety) just because REBT theory clearly distinguishes between healthy and unhealthy negative emotions. Do not forget that REBT theory is a guide to your interventions with your client who, generally speaking, knows little or nothing about this theory when they seek your help. In particular, your client may have in mind the goal of feeling calm in the face of threat or getting rid of the threat altogether. It is your job to help him see that setting feeling concern when confronted by threat as an initial goal will enable him to take constructive steps to deal with the threat and will enable him to stand back and determine whether his threat-related inferences are accurate or distorted.

Discussing emotional goals with your client is particularly relevant when dealing with unhealthy anger and guilt, although as DiGiuseppe (1988) has noted clients may think that they are supposed to feel a range of unhealthy negative emotions in response to particular types of negative activating event. When considering your client's anger problem, it is useful to assume that he doesn't distinguish between healthy anger and unhealthy anger, or, if he does make such a distinction, it is different from that made by REBT theory. Consequently, it is helpful for you to show your client what the behavioural and cognitive consequences of his healthy anger-based rational beliefs are and to contrast these favourably with the behavioural and cognitive consequences of his unhealthy anger-based irrational beliefs. Unless your client can see what the behavioural and thinking consequences of healthy anger-based rational beliefs are, and that it is in his interests to adopt them, he will not seek healthy anger as an emotional goal. This is also true if he does not see that his feelings of healthy anger can be strong, which they can be according to REBT theory. Thus, in many cases – and particularly where he considers anger (of some sort) to be a justified response to a negative activating event – your client will only accept healthy anger as a goal when it is a strong internal experience. To conclude, when your client has a problem of unhealthy anger, help him to see that healthy anger can be strong, but can lead to constructive behavioural and subsequent thinking responses.

When your client has a guilt problem, then it may be that he does not understand the difference between guilt (an unhealthy negative emotion based on an irrational belief about sins of commission or omission and/or hurting the feelings of another) and remorse (a healthy negative emotion based on a rational belief about similar inferred activating events). It is useful to teach your client this distinction and to show him that these different emotions (based as they are on different beliefs) have different behavioural and cognitive consequences. If you do not do this then your client may view your attempts to help him to give up his guilt as an attempt to condone his wrongdoing, for example, which he will resist.

So far we have discussed the importance of developing agreed healthy emotional goals with your client. It is also important that you develop agreed behavioural and cognitive goals with your client. With respect to behavioural goals, healthy actions are behaviours that aid your client in the achievement of his basic goals and purposes, and that are within your client's sphere of influence. Such behaviours may lead others to change, but the alteration of other people's behaviour should not be set as a goal with your client since this is not within your client's control.

Cognitive goals represent thinking consequences of rational beliefs, and as such they are realistic rather than positive in nature. As a consequence, you may have to disabuse clients who want you to help them to think positively. Help such clients to see that positive thinking in response to negative activating events is unrealistic and that realistic thinking in response to the same events is balanced, flexible and includes positive, negative and neutral outcomes.

Finally, it is important to help your client to see that emotional, behavioural and cognitive goals go together in what may be called an integrated goal package and, as such, you should ideally encourage your client to work towards the total package of goals rather than behavioural, emotional or cognitive goals in isolation from one another.

The task domain

Different systems of therapy suggest different tasks for therapist and client to carry out in the service of the client's goals. You can facilitate psychotherapeutic change in the task domain by:

- Helping your client to understand what his tasks are in the REBT process and eliciting agreement from him to carry out these tasks.
- Helping your client to understand how executing his tasks will help him to achieve his therapeutic goals.
- Training your client to carry out his tasks. This is particularly important when you employ written self-help forms. My (WD) custom is to deliberately train my clients in the self-help forms I suggest that they use, and to give them a worked example that serves as a model for good practice.
- Encouraging your client to carry out tasks in therapy that are within his range of competence. This means not suggesting that your client carry out tasks which are either too difficult for him or overly simplistic for him.
- Encouraging your client to understand and implement the work ethic in therapy. This ethic points to the fact that clients will gain most from therapy when they put the most into therapy. In this case, by implementing what they learn in therapy sessions outside therapy sessions.
- Helping your client to understand what your tasks in therapy are, why you are implementing them and how they relate to his therapeutic tasks.
- Executing your tasks in a skilful manner. REBT is an approach to therapy that is easy to practise poorly. Consequently, one of your responsibilities is to ensure that you are properly trained in REBT and that you submit yourself to regular supervision of your counselling work. From a skills-based perspective, it is important that you play your supervisor portions of tape-recordings of your therapy sessions so that he or she can give you feedback on your REBT skills. In addition, it is useful to undergo regular self-supervision of your audio-tapes (see Yapp & Dryden, 1994 for a framework to help you structure your self-supervision).
- Using a wide rather than a restricted range of tasks. The more REBT techniques you can master the more likely it is that you are going to help a wider range of clients, since different clients respond better to different techniques. Bernard and Wolfe (2000) have edited a very useful practitioner's resource manual containing the favourite techniques of the world's leading REBT therapists.
- Using tasks that are potent enough to address your client's problems and help him to achieve his goals. One of the biggest dangers in the technical practice of REBT is over-use of cognitive techniques and under-use of behavioural techniques. Thus, for a number of client problems, in particular anxiety-based problems, the use of cognitive techniques on their own is insufficient to promote client change. Our advice is, whenever possible, use conjoint cognitive-behavioural techniques, where your client acts in ways that are consistent with developing rational beliefs while mentally rehearsing these beliefs.

Initiating the working relationship

In initiating the working relationship with your client it is important that you encourage your client to tell you, in his own way, about his problems and what he wants to achieve from consulting you. In responding to him it is important that you communicate your understanding of his problems from his point of view, as well helping him to see that there is a different, more constructive way in which he can see, and therefore deal with his problems. Throughout this early phase of therapy, it is important that you encourage your client to feel comfortable enough to tell you exactly what is on his mind. It is also important that you convey confidence, not only in your role as REBT therapist, but also in your ability to help your client.

The early phase of REBT is the time when you explain briefly the nature of this approach to therapy and socialise your client into REBT. This involves stressing the active–directive, problem-focused nature of this approach, and that it requires your client to participate actively in this process, and to put into practice outside therapy sessions what he learns inside these sessions.

As soon as possible, it is important that you introduce your client to the ABC model and help him to use this model to address specific examples of his target problems. Then, you will show him how to dispute the irrational beliefs that you have encouraged him to identify while using the ABC model. The early phase of REBT is characterised by dealing with specific examples of your client's problems but, as you do this, you will be formulating hypotheses about his core irrational beliefs, which you will deal with more directly in the middle phase of therapy.

Maintaining the working relationship

In order to maintain the working relationship that you have established with your client, it is important to follow through on problems that you have begun to work on in the beginning phase of REBT. Helping your client to generalise his gains from one example of a target problem to other examples of this problem is one important way that you can do this. You can then switch the therapeutic focus to your client's other problems and show him how he can apply what he has learned from working on target problem 1 to target problem 2. As we will discuss later, a particularly efficient way of doing this is to teach your client specific REBT change-related skills, such as assessing specific problems and disputing irrational beliefs.

As you continue to work on your client's specific problems, you will begin to construct an overall picture of your client and his problems and in particular, the irrational beliefs that underpin these problems. These beliefs are known as core irrational beliefs and work on these beliefs is a key aspect of the middle phase of REBT. In addition, you will begin to identify ways in which your client wittingly and unwittingly perpetuates his problems (perhaps by employing a variety of safety-seeking manoeuvres designed to keep him safe in the short term, but which have the effect of perpetuating his problems in the longer term), and help him to develop more constructive responses.

As your client works to relinquish irrational beliefs – both specific and core – and to acquire rational alternatives to these beliefs, he will encounter a variety of obstacles to change. While dealing with such obstacles is a major task for you as a therapist throughout the REBT therapeutic process, it is particularly salient in the middle phase of therapy. This is a time when the honeymoon period is over and the client realises that only hard work and confronting his problems over time will enable him to achieve his therapeutic objectives. Helping your client to maintain therapeutic momentum is important if your client is to remain in therapy and achieve long-term benefits from the process.

One key way to help your client to maintain his therapeutic momentum involves you keeping the focus of the therapy on his goals. It is easy for your client to move from topic to topic and from problem to problem if you allow him to do so, and thus maintaining a focus is important in REBT. While at the beginning of REBT the focus is on dealing with one target problem at a time, the focus in the middle phase is best placed on your client's goals, particularly when he has made some progress in dealing with his problems. Keeping a goal-oriented focus enables your client to stay motivated and provides a rationale for him to tolerate the discomfort that invariably accompanies psychotherapeutic change. A reworking of the old adage 'no pains without gains' expresses this well: 'It is worth putting up with the pains in order to achieve the gains.'

Another important way to encourage your client to maintain his therapeutic momentum involves you helping him to prevent relapse and deal with vulnerability factors. In doing so, it is important to help your client see that lapses are an inevitable part of psychotherapeutic change, and that adopting a rational attitude towards a lapse and dealing with it effectively helps to prevent a lapse becoming a relapse.

From the outset of therapy, REBT therapists are increasingly teaching REBT techniques to their clients, in order that the latter can use these skills for themselves. However, well into the middle phase of counselling, you should place the issue of encouraging your client to become his own counsellor centre stage. Maxie C. Maultsby Jr, the well known pioneer of a related therapy known as 'Rational Behaviour Therapy', was once quoted as saying that counselling only works to the extent to which the client uses what he learns in the counselling room. This, then, places the responsibility for maintaining psychotherapeutic change squarely on your client's shoulders. Having said that, your primary responsibility on this issue is to do all you can to encourage your client to assume this responsibility. This means that as the REBT therapy process unfolds and as your client makes progress, you encourage him to take the lead during therapy sessions by using the REBT framework to assess his own problems, dispute his own irrational beliefs and make his own suggestions concerning how he can strengthen his rational beliefs.

Ending the working relationship

REBT is not an endless, open-ended process. As an REBT therapist one of your goals is to equip your clients with the knowledge and skills that mean they can become their own therapist in order that they can help themselves in the future. Given this, it is important that you work towards ending therapy in a way that best facilitates clients assuming the responsibility for continuing self-care. The following will help you manage this important transition.

1 *Decide on how and when to end.* While REBT therapists do not consider that most clients need to work through at great length their feelings about ending therapy, we do consider that ending therapy is an important event for clients and that discussion concerning how and when to end therapy needs to be carried out as soon as both parties agree that the process of REBT is nearing its end. With most of my clients, I (WD) work on the principle of decreasing contact, in that we increase the period between sessions. A common ending of this nature is as follows:

   once a week → once every two weeks → once a month → once every
   two months → once every three months → once every six months

   At this point, therapy is effectively at an end and the client is in follow-up mode.
   This is only one way of ending the process and some clients prefer a definite ending date with no further contact unless initiated by the client. The important point about deciding how and when to end is that these matters are discussed fully with clients before a joint decision is made.

2 *Encourage your client to summarise what he has learned.* As you and your client approach the end of your work together it is useful to ask him to summarise what he has learned from therapy. Doing so provides you with an opportunity to:

   • correct any last-minute misconceptions that your client may have about what he has learned or about REBT;
   • help your client to remember important lessons for future reference;
   • take what your client has learned and discuss ways in which he can continue to capitalise on learning.

Some clients find it helpful to keep a written summary of what they have learned and periodically to review this summary even if they are not experiencing any problems. This helps reinforce the idea that one has to do something to maintain one's therapeutic gains.

3 *Attribute improvement to your clients' efforts.* When reviewing what your clients have learned from therapy, you may find that some of them attribute all they have gained to your efforts. Tempting as it may be to bathe in such glory, it is important that you resist such a temptation.

4 *Deal with obstacles to ending.*

5 *Agree on criteria for follow-ups and for resuming therapy.*

We will consider the initiating, maintaining and ending phases of therapy again in the final chapter when we consider the process of therapy.

Educating the client

Albert Ellis (1994) has argued that a major task REBT therapists have is to educate their clients on a variety of issues concerning the nature of psychological disturbance, how it is acquired and perpetuated, and how it can be changed. Before we list a sample of topics which are frequently the focus for such education, it is important to stress from the outset that REBT is not prescriptive when it comes to the educational styles adopted by its therapists, although it is important to note that in general, an active–directive educational style is preferred to a more passive, non-directive style. Here then is a representative sample of topics that REBT therapists teach their clients.

Teaching the ABCs of REBT

The essence of REBT is contained in the ABC model – namely that people disturb themselves about negative critical activating events by the rigid and extreme beliefs (irrational beliefs) that they hold about these events. If you don't teach the ABC model at all then your clients will continue to think that events themselves cause their disturbed feelings. And if you teach your clients the ABC model but without sufficient care or clarity then they may plausibly, but incorrectly, think that their inferences largely account for their disturbed feelings.

You should endeavour to teach all your clients that their irrational beliefs at B largely determine their unhealthy negative emotions and their self-defeating behaviour at C, but you can also show your more intellectual and sophisticated clients that these irrational beliefs also have a great impact on their subsequent unrealistic thinking at C.

While it is important to teach clients the ABCs of psychological disturbance, it is equally important to teach them the ABCs of psychological health and, in particular, that such health in the face of adversities is best facilitated by flexible and non-extreme beliefs about these negative events. It is particularly relevant to help clients keenly discriminate between irrational beliefs and their rational beliefs. This involves showing clients the difference between partial and full versions of rational beliefs (see Chapter 1).

Teaching clients which inferences feature in their emotional problems

It is useful to teach your clients which inferences are involved in their emotional problems but, as noted above, it is important to do this without inadvertently teaching them that inferences alone account for their unhealthy negative emotions. Once a client has understood which inferences feature in their problems (in their critical As), he can check for the presence of such a theme if he is unclear what he is disturbed about in a given situation. Figure 1.5 lists the major themes associated with different unhealthy negative emotions. However, you should use the information contained in this figure as a launch pad for the identification of your client's idiosyncratic, recurring inferences.

Teaching rational principles

REBT has a unique perspective on a number of therapeutic issues and as such it is important that you teach your clients the REBT view on relevant issues. For example, REBT has a particular stance on a topic that is relevant for many clients – self-esteem. It holds that unconditional self-acceptance is a healthier position for clients to strive towards than self-esteem. In order for your clients to understand this position fully you need to teach them the rational principle of unconditional self-acceptance:

- The self is everything about a person that can be rated (Hauck, 1991).
- The self is too complex to be rated and is made up of good, bad and neutral aspects.
- While you cannot legitimately rate your 'self', you can rate discrete aspects of yourself and what happens to you.
- Human beings are by nature fallible and cannot be perfected.
- Humans beings are constantly in process, while ratings of 'self' are static.
- All humans are equal in shared humanity, but unequal in many specific aspects.
- Healthy self-acceptance is unconditional.
- Unconditional self-acceptance is founded on non-dogmatic preferences.
- Unconditional self-acceptance promotes healthy emotions and constructive behaviour.
- Acceptance does not mean resignation. Thus, when you accept yourself you are encouraged to change what you don't like about yourself.

- Self-acceptance is not a perfectly achievable state, never to be lost once attained. Rather, developing self-acceptance is a process.

Teaching the REBT perspective on psychotherapeutic change

Another topic that REBT therapists teach their clients is the REBT perspective on psychotherapeutic change so that clients can understand what they need to do to overcome their problems (see Chapter 3 for a detailed discussions of these steps).

Structuring the psychotherapeutic process

As we discussed earlier in this chapter, REBT is primarily an active–directive approach to psychotherapy. One of the important aspects of this approach is that, as a therapist, you take the lead in structuring therapy for the client. You don't do this unilaterally, but with the client's permission, once you have explained what you plan to do and why. If you don't structure the process, you will be following the client's lack of structure and this will not enable you to practise REBT effectively. The following will assist you in helping your client effectively:

- Being structured in developing a list of problems and goals.
- Being structured in helping your client select one problem at a time to work with (the 'target' problem).
- Being structured in working with specific examples of target problems.
- Being structured in using the ABC framework to assess problems.
- Being structured when disputing your client's irrational beliefs.
- Being structured when negotiating and reviewing homework assignments.
- Being structured in helping your client to identify and challenge core irrational beliefs.
- Being structured in dealing with obstacles to change.
- Being structured in helping your client to prevent relapse.
- Being structured in helping your client to become his own therapist.

Two further points with respect to structure are important. First, as the therapeutic process develops, you will want to encourage your client to take more responsibility in using the structure of REBT in therapy sessions as a prelude to him using this structure for himself outside sessions. Second, there will be times when you will want to be less structured with your clients – for example, when a client discloses, with distress, material that he has not told anyone before. Effective REBT therapists are flexible in their use of the structure of REBT.

Assessing your client's problems accurately

An accurate assessment of your client's problems is a precursor to psychotherapeutic change. Assessment in REBT is done at two major levels: the problem level and the client level. Let us first consider assessment at the problem level. Here, a careful assessment is made of specific client problems and goals with respect to these problems. You first encourage your client to choose one problem to work on (the 'target' problem). Then you ask for a specific example of this problem to assess. In doing so, you assess:

- Your client's dysfunctional Cs (emotional, behavioural and cognitive) in the situation in question.
- The aspect of the situation about which your client was most disturbed (the critical A).
- Your client's specific irrational beliefs.
- What your client does and thinks (usually unwittingly) to maintain the problem. In particular, safety-seeking behaviours and cognitions are considered.
- Your client's realistic goals for change, ensuring that you elicit emotional, behavioural and – where relevant – cognitive goals for change.
- Any relevant obstacles to change that will prevent your client from dealing constructively with his problem.

Now let us consider REBT assessment at the level of the client. This involves developing an accurate understanding of the person in the context of his problems or UPCP (Dryden, 1998), which is referred to as a case formulation or case conceptualisation in other approaches to cognitive psychotherapy (Bruch & Bond, 1998; Persons, 1989). While a full discussion of this issue is outside the scope of this book, REBT therapists conduct a formal UPCP with complex 'cases', or when they are stuck with a client. They also use aspects of a UPCP in their everyday practice.

Skilfully implementing REBT strategies and techniques

Effective REBT therapists implement REBT strategies and techniques skilfully and creatively. In order to do this, they are fully and professionally trained in the theory and practice of REBT, receive regular supervision and engage in ongoing self-supervision (Yapp & Dryden, 1994). In order to develop and sharpen their skills, effective REBT therapists make tape-recordings of their therapy sessions and periodically present these to their supervisors for feedback on their use of REBT skills.

Teaching REBT skills to clients and facilitating their learning of these skills

Ultimately, the effectiveness of REBT depends on clients learning REBT self-therapy skills and regularly applying these skills after therapy has formally ended. As an REBT therapist, your major role here is both to teach your clients these skills and to do all you can to ensure that they learn them. I (WD) have written a client workbook that aims to teach clients the most important skills of REBT in a formal and structured way (Dryden, 2001). In this workbook I explain each skill in detail, give precise step-by-step instructions in its use, provide a specific example of the skill being used, and explain how common mistakes in the application of the skill can be avoided. Then, in therapy, I go over the client's use of each skill and provide relevant feedback to improve skill development.

It is important to note that while you are responsible for teaching clients REBT skills, doing all you can to help them learn the skills, and teaching clients how to tackle the obstacles to using these skills in their daily life, ultimately you are not responsible for whether clients use these skills or not.

Encouraging generalisation

There are a number of points that you need to keep in mind when encouraging your clients to generalise their gains.

Facing specific situations and focusing on critical As is important

As your client begins to generalise his psychotherapeutic gains, it is important that you encourage him to face relevant situations and, in particular as he does so, to focus on the critical A within the situation. Otherwise, he may well distract himself and gain emotional relief as a result. You should realise that clients sometimes have very subtle and covert ways of avoiding facing their critical As and of avoiding experiencing their disturbed feelings as a result. Consequently, if you are to help your clients generalise their psychotherapeutic gains you need to be alert to these distraction strategies and to encourage your clients to drop them and to face up to their critical As and the unhealthy negative emotions that they will experience as a result. In this way, they will gain valuable experience of practising to think rationally in the face of their critical As across different situations.

Encourage your clients to rehearse rational beliefs in a deliberate manner

According to REBT theory, rational beliefs are the cornerstone of psychological health. Consequently, if you are to help your clients achieve their healthy goals then the most robust way of doing so is by encouraging them to develop and deepen their conviction in their rational beliefs. So, as you help your clients generalise their therapeutic gains you should actively look for ways of helping them to think rationally in each relevant situation.

The most reliable way of ensuring that your clients gain valuable practise at thinking rationally in the relevant situations, while focusing on relevant critical As, is by encouraging them to rehearse their developing rational beliefs in a deliberate fashion. If you leave it to chance that they will rehearse their rational beliefs, or if you work on the assumption that they will naturally generalise thinking rationally from one situation to the next, then you may well be doing your clients a disservice. Our own experience has been that with most clients – certainly at the beginning of the generalisation process – you need to encourage them to rehearse their rational beliefs in a deliberate way as they face relevant new situations. Initially, you can suggest that they say their rational beliefs out loud (when other people are not present) in relevant situations; then, they can rehearse them *sotto voce*, and finally they can review their rational beliefs silently in their head, while all the time facing the relevant critical As embedded in the physical situations which provide the context for the generalisation of their psychotherapeutic gains.

The holy trinity: the importance of rehearsing rational beliefs while acting constructively and thinking realistically

Perhaps the most powerful way of promoting psychotherapeutic generalisation is to encourage your clients to rehearse their newly developed rational beliefs in relevant situations while acting and thinking in ways that are consistent with these beliefs. This involves you helping your clients identify ways in which they act and think which are consistent with their *irrational* beliefs and, after encouraging them to dispute these beliefs, helping them to select behaviours and thoughts that directly counter this dysfunctional behaviour and unrealistic thinking. If your clients can use the holy trinity of rehearsing irrational beliefs, acting constructively and thinking realistically across relevant situations then they will make most progress in generalising their psychotherapeutic gains.

Figure 4.1 lists different combinations of belief–behaviour–thinking configurations and their power to facilitate psychotherapeutic generalisation across relevant situations. Note that 'CWRB' stands for 'consistent with rational belief' and 'CWIB' stands for 'consistent with irrational belief'.

Figure 4.1 shows that behaviour which is consistent with rational beliefs is more powerful in facilitating psychotherapeutic generalisation than subsequent thinking that is thus also consistent in facilitating psychotherapeutic generalisation, because it has more power to strengthen these rational beliefs. Conversely, this figure also shows that behaviour which is consistent with irrational beliefs is more powerful in

Figure 4.1   Combinations of belief–behaviour–thinking configurations with their power to facilitate psychotherapeutic generalisation listed in descending order

Rational belief – constructive behaviour (CWRB) – realistic thinking (CWRB)
Rational belief – constructive behaviour (CWRB) – unrealistic thinking (CWIB)
Rational belief – unconstructive behaviour (CWIB) – realistic thinking (CWRB)
Rational belief – unconstructive behaviour (CWIB) – unrealistic thinking (CWIB)
Irrational belief – constructive behaviour (CWRB) – realistic thinking (CWRB)
Irrational belief – constructive behaviour (CWRB) – unrealistic thinking (CWIB)
Irrational belief – unconstructive behaviour (CWIB) – realistic thinking (CWRB)
Irrational belief – unconstructive behaviour (CWIB) – unrealistic thinking (CWIB)

'CWRB' = Consistent with rational beliefs
'CWIB' = Consistent with irrational beliefs

preventing psychotherapeutic generalisation than subsequent thinking that is also thus consistent in preventing psychotherapeutic generalisation because it has more power to strengthen these irrational beliefs. Finally, Figure 4.1 shows that when you successfully encourage your clients to rehearse rational beliefs while at the same time acting and thinking in ways that are consistent with rational beliefs, then this is the best way to facilitate psychotherapeutic generalisation.

Action is better than imagery in promoting therapeutic generalisation, but imagery may make action more likely

As we have just stated, behaviour that is consistent with rational beliefs is a particularly potent way of strengthening these rational beliefs and thus promoting psychotherapeutic generalisation. However, taking such action while facing negative activating events can be quite discomfiting and many clients would prefer to face these As in their imagination. While behaviour is more powerful than imagery in promoting psychotherapeutic generalisation, you may be more likely to encourage your clients to take such action if you first have them face relevant negative activating events in their mind's eye.

Helping clients to prevent relapse

Once your clients have made progress in overcoming their problems and you have helped them to generalise their gains, then you need to help them to prevent relapse. We define a lapse as a temporary and non-serious return to a problem state while a relapse is a more enduring, more serious return to that state. In order to help your clients prevent a relapse you need to do the following:

1 Help your clients review what they have learned in therapy.
2 Help them think through how they can apply what they have learned to future problems.
3 Help them identify factors to which they remain vulnerable.
4 Help them determine how they would deal constructively with these vulnerability factors should they encounter them.
5 Encourage them to put this constructive plan into action by facing their vulnerability factors.
6 Help them review their experiences of dealing with these vulnerability factors and learn from such reviews accordingly.
7 Help them to develop rational beliefs about lapses.
8 Help them learn from these lapses.
9 Help them to develop rational beliefs about relapse.
10 Help them learn from a relapse, should one occur.
11 Help them to continue to identify and overcome obstacles to maintaining psychotherapeutic change.
12 Encourage them to make practising the self-help methods of REBT an integral part of their future self-care regime.

Helping clients overcome obstacles to change

Therapy of whatever persuasion rarely goes smoothly, and effective REBT therapists anticipate that their clients will experience a variety of obstacles to psychotherapeutic change. They also help these clients to accept this grim reality without disturbing themselves about it and to address these obstacles in an effective problem-solving manner. We will deal with this topic fully in Chapter 6.

Having considered the therapist's role in promoting client change in REBT, in the next chapter we will consider the client's role in promoting psychotherapeutic change.

In this chapter we discuss the client's role in REBT and what he needs to do if he is to achieve a successful outcome to his problems. Some clients might think they are being given a job description when you talk about their role and responsibilities in therapy (there is indeed quite a lot of work for clients to undertake both in and between sessions, and after therapy has ended). However one looks at it, clients do have a job of work to do, although how you communicate this will vary from client to client. What does not vary, however, is that REBT teaches clients the skills to become their own therapist, but this is dependent upon them accepting the 'job description' and investing their role in therapy with determination and energy.

Complying with the 'demand' characteristics of REBT

In this context, demand does not mean 'must adhere to' but 'highly desirable to adhere to'. The demand characteristics of REBT include: collaboration, structured sessions, use of the ABCDE model, a problem focus largely in the here and now, homework assignments, specific and realistic goals (some of these demand characteristics are discussed later in the chapter). The general point we wish to make is that working in a structured, focused and specific way is crucial if your clients are to gain maximum benefit from REBT. Clients who have been in non-directive forms of therapy are likely to experience REBT as a 'culture shock'; other clients may become irritated with your questions directing them to the salient aspects of their problems when they want to expatiate upon them without frequent interruptions from you.

In order to defuse such difficulties, early in the first session explain the basics of REBT, so that clients can decide if they wish to proceed with this form of therapy. If your client gives you his informed consent to proceed, then you can discuss in greater detail, when appropriate, what REBT requires from him if he is to realise his goals. His consent initiates his role in REBT.

Describing problems clearly and concisely

Clients may provide you with a lot of information about their problems, but some or even most of this information may be irrelevant from the REBT viewpoint (such as lengthy biographies of other people connected to the client's problems). Also, clients may talk about their problems in vague ways such as 'It's something around speaking up in groups.'

What is required from clients is clear and specific information about their presenting problems in order for you to undertake an ABC assessment of them. With regard to 'It's something around speaking up in groups', a specific understanding of the problem would be:

Situational A = Imagining speaking up in a group.
Critical A = Being laughed at by other group members for making 'stupid comments'.
B = 'I must not be laughed at by other group members for making stupid comments because I could not stand to be seen as stupid.'
C = Anxiety.

In REBT, the focus is on eliciting B, not extended discussions of A or C. Encouraging clients to describe their problems in succinct ways (which you can model for them), helps them to use the ABC framework through which to view, discuss and understand their problems. Providing concise and clear information prevents clients from becoming entangled in the thickets of long-winded explanations of their problems. If a client has a number of problems to discuss, he can draw up a problem list with a realistic goal established for each problem. The client's key role in problem assessment is to use the ABC model to understand his problems and discuss them clearly and concisely, with his main focus on uncovering the B – as this, not A, is the chief determinant of emotional disturbance at C.

Focusing largely on the here and now

REBT's primary focus is on how current problems are being maintained rather than on how these problems were acquired. The client might believe that the cause of his problem and its solution lie in the past (this view might be held because of the client's previous experiences of therapy or popular views of what therapy entails). As Grieger and Boyd explain:

Human emotional problems do not result from the experiences people have, whether these experiences are historical or current, but from the way people interpret and continue to interpret these experiences. When a person is emotionally disturbed, the disturbance results from a currently held way of thinking and behaving. It is usually true that the client's irrational ideas have a learning history, but the crucial thing is for him or her to give up these currently held ideas so that tomorrow's existence can be better than yesterday's. (1980: 76–7)

While REBT is mainly present-centred, it does not prevent the client from looking back at past events, but discourages him from dwelling there. The client can learn to link past experiences with present problems (for example, 'I still feel angry today about my father walking out on us when I was 10 years old'). The client's focus should mainly be on discussing present problems and revealing the irrational beliefs that maintain them. Looking back is used productively by the client to understand how he still disturbs himself today about past events because he continues to subscribe to irrational beliefs about these events.

Making a commitment to change

When your client states his goals for change, this does not automatically mean that he has committed himself to undertaking the hard work to realise these goals. Clients may have idiosyncratic definitions of what commitment means (such as, 'I don't mind trying to change as long as things do not get too difficult for me'). In order to crystallise the issue of commitment from the outset of REBT, this is one analogy we often use: 'You want to complete the London marathon which is in nine months' time and you are currently unfit. In order to have a good chance of crossing the finishing line, you need to start training now, and on a regular basis, to acquire the fitness and stamina needed for the race. Can you see the point I'm making with regard to overcoming your problems?' Grieger states that effecting change is 'a 24-hour-a-day, seven-day-a-week thing' (1991: 60). While this may be an extreme position to take, it can be used as a yardstick by your clients to measure their commitment to change. Commitment means the client doing whatever it takes to overcome his self-defeating thoughts, feelings and behaviours, while 'commitment with qualifiers' ('I will do whatever it takes provided it doesn't take too long') means that change is likely to fall short of the client's desired goals. The client needs to commit himself without qualifiers to the change process if he wants to realise his desired goals. This commitment can be expressed succinctly in the client's own words, in phrases such as 'Keep pushing forward', 'Never give up.'

Acting as a collaborator in the change process

Change is more likely to occur when clients act in tandem with you rather than relying on you for change to occur. From the earliest possible opportunity in therapy, start emphasising 'working together' to disabuse clients of any ideas they may have that REBT will be a passive experience for them (i.e. that you will resolve their problems for them without them having to do any work apart from attending the session and listening to you). Acting as a collaborator helps clients to gain both confidence and competence in the problem-solving process and shows them that their contributions to therapy are valued by you.

As a team, you and your client will work together closely to identify problems, define goals and find the means to achieve these goals. As the client's skill as a problem-solver increases, he becomes more independent in therapy (with you relegated to the role of a coach or consultant) and takes the lead in shaping therapy sessions: setting the agenda, taking himself through the ABC model with minimal prompting from you, questioning his irrational beliefs, designing homework tasks, etc. The client's view of himself in therapy moves from collaborator to self-therapist.

Being open to the REBT framework

This entails the client's willingness to be open to the REBT viewpoint in explaining his problems; namely, that our emotional problems are largely self-induced, not caused by others or events. In particular, the client needs to consider carefully three key REBT insights which explain the development, maintenance and amelioration of emotional problems (Neenan & Dryden, 2000):

1   Human disturbance is largely determined by irrational beliefs. To paraphrase Epictetus, a Stoic philosopher from the first century AD: 'People are disturbed not by things, but by their rigid and extreme views of things.'
2   We remain disturbed in the present because we continually reindoctrinate or brainwash ourselves with these beliefs and act in ways that strengthen them.
3   The only enduring way to overcome our emotional problems is through persistent hard work and practice – to think, feel and act against our irrational beliefs.

We are not suggesting that your clients simply accept what you say, but that they be open-minded enough to 'chew over' the merit of your ideas while raising some objections to or reservations about these ideas. In this way, an open and fruitful dialogue can develop about REBT, with you correcting any misconceptions that the client may have about it, such as, 'So I'm supposed to be rational at all times. Is that right?' Remaining sceptical (not in the cynical sense) about REBT while engaging in the practice of it, is not a self-defeating stance to take: progress can occur despite the client's doubts. If the client has a fixed view on the reasons for her problems and how to solve them ('My husband makes me unhappy and he has to treat me better if I'm to feel better') and will not consider the REBT viewpoint, then little progress will be made.

Clients need to view their thoughts and beliefs as hypotheses about reality rather than as true representations of reality, in other words, learning to act as a personal scientist by reality-testing their beliefs, evaluating data objectively and drawing conclusions from them. For example, a client who believes that he must have a partner in order to be happy, can engage in a series of experiments to reality-test his belief and thereby realise that while a partner is highly desirable, he still can be relatively happy without one. Beliefs as 'facts' can seem immutable whereas beliefs as hypotheses are open to challenge and change and thereby lead to an improvement in the client's present functioning.

Thinking SMART and hard about goals

Your client may suggest goals which he has not thought carefully about – for example, 'I want my boss to treat me better.' This goal lies within his boss's control, not the client's. One method of introducing rigour into goal selection is to think 'SMART'. Is the client's goal:

- Simple and Specific (e.g. 'I want a relationship with a woman')?
- Measurable (e.g. 'I will ask two woman out each week until I get a firm date')?
- Agreed (you are willing to go along with the goal)?
- Realistic (it is within the client's current ability to achieve it)?
- Timebound (the goal is achievable within the time the client is prepared to spend in therapy)?

Clients may choose goals of feeling relaxed about, indifferent or resigned to negative life events. Feeling relaxed might mean not taking constructive action to tackle adverse events (like being in debt), being indifferent usually means the client is suppressing his rational desires for bad events not to have occurred (like the end of a relationship), and being resigned to the inevitability of one's fate (like eternal solitude) is only likely to occur if the client is not prepared to create a different future for himself by thinking and acting differently. When you and your client agree on goals, ensure they do not reinforce the client's problems.

Clients might select goals that are unrealistically ambitious (for example, 'To never worry again') or unrealistically unambitious ('Just to scrape through in my exams'). With the latter goal, goal theory suggests that challenging goals produce a better performance than easy or underwhelming goals. We suggest that clients strive for goals that are challenging, but not overwhelming – they should be sufficiently stimulating to promote therapeutic change through persistent effort, but not so daunting as to inhibit clients from achieving them.

We encourage clients to consider two types of goals: i) goals that relate to overcoming psychological problems (OPP); and ii) goals that relate to personal development (PD). We stress to our clients that the best way of achieving personal development goals is by first achieving the goal of overcoming psychological problems. For example, a client now feels healthy instead of unhealthy anger when criticised by others; his PD goal is to focus on the validity of the criticisms rather than on the person who made them. Some clients believe that they can move straight to the PD goal and bypass the OPP one, but this is unrealistic and inadvisable as their disturbance-inducing beliefs will still be intact and, therefore, are highly likely to undermine their attempts to realise PD goals.

The client's role in determining his goals is to use the SMART criteria, follow the principle of challenging for him – but not overwhelming for him – and realise and accept that achieving OPP goals comes before consideration of any PD goals he may have in mind.

Accepting emotional responsibility

Clients often blame 'he/she/it' for causing their problems ('A-C thinking', as REBT calls it). If this view of emotional causation persists in therapy, clients will continue to believe that emotional relief is delivered by others instead of themselves. Accepting emotional responsibility (B-C thinking) means that the client sees himself as the primary agent of his emotional disturbance with others contributing to it, but not causing it. This shift in emotional causation needs to be reinforced in the client's language, for example, 'I make myself angry when I don't get my own way' or 'I create my own anxiety by demanding that things must go perfectly.'

While this new way of thinking and speaking will seem strange to clients long used to A-C ways of responding to events, it is vital that they engage in it if they are to take control of their emotional destiny. It is important that the client does not equate responsibility with blame: responsibility is acknowledging largely self-induced disturbance while blame is fault-finding or self-censure ('I'm weak for having anxiety problems').

You can help your clients to accept emotional responsibility by i) pointing out that people have different reactions to the same event, so the event cannot be responsible for their feelings, otherwise everyone would feel the same: does being stuck in a traffic jam 'make' everyone angry?; and ii) if feelings are 'given' to us by others, you can try to give some feelings to your client such as 'I want you to feel really happy now' which the client is likely to reject as he does not appraise his current circumstances as happiness-inducing.

How clients feel is based on their evaluation of events: rigid and extreme evaluations of events (e.g. 'I absolutely should not have lost my job, and as I did, I'm worthless without one') often lead to unhealthy negative emotions, such as depression, whereas flexible and non-extreme evaluations of events (e.g. 'I would greatly prefer not to have lost my job but there is no reason why I must not lose it. Having lost it has no bearing on my worth as a person. I'm a person with less in my life, but not less of a person') usually produce healthy negative emotions, such as sadness.

If your client is to internalise emotional responsibility, it is crucial he uses B-C language and tolerates the newness and strangeness of talking in this way while simultaneously struggling against his natural tendency to use A-C language; he does not confuse responsibility with blame; and sees that his emotions belong to him, no one else: they are not given to him by others.

Accepting therapeutic responsibility

Accepting emotional responsibility does not remove emotional distur-bance, but only underscores personal ownership of the problem. Removing emotional disturbance occurs through multimodal (cognitive, an imagined, behavioural and emotive) disputing of the disturbance-producing beliefs, in the situations in which they arise. In other words, clients are required to undertake a programme of work in order to effect change in their life. Accepting therapeutic responsibility means the client under-stands that you can show them what needs to be done, but you cannot do it for them. An analogy can help some clients to grasp this point: 'Your GP might recommend some exercises to ease your stiff back, but you, not she, are the only person who can carry out the exercises.'

Disputing irrational beliefs is probably the most important activity that clients engage in. As Hauck states: 'In all counselling, one task is more critical than any other. It is self-debate. Throughout your counseling it is practically always critical that you keep the client oriented toward ques-tioning, challenging, and debating with himself over his irrational ideas' (1980: 244).

Therapist-initiated debate promotes client self-debate. Irrational beliefs (for example, 'I must not make mistakes because if I do this proves I'm incompetent') are disputed in five major ways, focusing on:

1   Rigidity vs. flexibility – the client's belief, 'I must not make mistakes', is rigid because it does not allow for the possibility of making mistakes or acknowledging previous ones and assumes that human behaviour can be strictly controlled.
2   Extreme or non-extreme – the client's conclusion 'I'm incompetent' (for making mistakes) is extreme because it does not recognize the fallibility and complexity of human beings – one aspect of the person is used to condemn the whole person.
3   Logic – because the person does not want to make mistakes, it does not logically follow that he must not make them, so the conclusion ('I'm incompetent') based on this premise is also false.
4   Empiricism – does the client's demand not to make mistakes correspond with empirical reality? The evidence shows that the client does make

mistakes. Also, if he truly was incompetent, then this is the only way he could act. The evidence contradicts this view of himself.

5 Pragmatism – does the client's irrational belief help him to attain his goal (learning from mistakes in order to make fewer of them)? What are the consequences for him of holding on to this belief? (Anxiety when anticipating making a mistake and anger and depression following the mistake.)

The client's rational alternative to the irrational belief (e.g. 'I would prefer not to make mistakes, but there is no reason why I must not make them. If I do, this proves I'm a fallible human being who can accept himself for making them') is not taken on trust, but subjected to the same five tests as the irrational belief in order to demonstrate that the new belief is flexible, non-extreme, logical, consistent with reality, and helpful.

Therapeutic responsibility is, in essence, your client entering problematic situations in his life and forcefully disputing his associated irrational beliefs in order to weaken them and strengthen his new rational beliefs by thinking and acting in constructive ways in these same situations.

Being aware of and dealing with meta-emotional problems

Meta-emotional problems are secondary problems about primary problems (such as being ashamed of feeling anxious, or being angry about feeling guilty) – clients give themselves two problems for the price of one. Clients need to be alert to the presence of meta-emotional problems as these may hinder their work and progress on the primary problem. For example, I (MN) saw a business executive whose self-image as a 'no-nonsense-get-on-with-it' high achiever was undermined by a series of panic attacks. Progress in tackling his panic was stalled by his intense shame about these attacks ('I'm utterly weak and completely pathetic for having them'). Only by tackling and overcoming his shame (meta-emotional problem) were we then able to return to our clinical focus on his panic attacks (primary problem). If your client detects a meta-emotional problem, then he needs to bring this to your attention for discussion of its priority: can it be dealt with later in therapy or should it be tackled immediately?

Realising that insight alone is insufficient to promote change

Some clients may believe that if they gain insight into the development of their problems ('Why am I like this?'), then their symptoms will spontaneously improve or their problems will disappear. Gaining insight may be described as phase one of the change process ('I can see that I have low self-esteem because my parents kept telling me I wouldn't amount to much in life and I continue to believe that'). Phase two would be developing an alternative self-image, based on self-acceptance and working hard to achieve more ambitious life goals. Phase three of the change process would be maintaining these gains over the long term.

We might say to our clients that what they see (insight) and do (sustained effort) brings lasting therapeutic change; what they see but do not do brings them very little except the consolation of insight. Therefore, it is important clients understand that REBT is an insight and action form of therapy. To remind themselves of this fact, clients might want to devise a saying, such as, 'Seeing and doing delivers the goods, while seeing without doing means the goods never arrive.'

Developing a philosophy of effort

Change usually comes at a price: in REBT terms, the hard work and continual practice involved in developing and maintaining new problem-solving skills. Little progress is likely to be made if your clients continue to adhere to an outlook based on low frustration tolerance (e.g., 'The hard work required of me to change my self-defeating beliefs and behaviours is too much to bear'). A philosophy of effort is enshrined in the maxim, 'There is rarely any gain without some pain.' As the pain comes before the gain, Ellis urges clients to court discomfort deliberately:

> So make yourself do the work you dislike, force yourself to do it and do it. Deliberately push yourself to be uncomfortable – yes, uncomfortable – until you finally find the work easy and comfortable. By courting and courting discomfort, and by that hard route alone, you'll later become comfortable. Not right away – later. (1985: 102)

When faced with the hard work ahead, some clients say, 'I'll try to do it', and thereby believe they have committed themselves to doing it. However, 'I'll try' indicates little personal responsibility and half-hearted attempts at change, while 'I'll do it' means the client is taking personal responsibility in order to get the results he is seeking in his life. Finding examples in the client's life where he is 'doing' and comparing these with examples where he is 'trying', can help him to highlight the attitudinal differences in these situations. Therefore, to achieve his goals, your client needs to adopt a 'doing' attitude underpinned by high frustration tolerance: 'I'll do the tasks and tolerate the intense discomfort I will experience while doing them.'

Carrying out homework assignments

If clients are coming to see you for one hour each week, what are they doing with the remaining 167 hours in the week? Homework puts the learning that has occurred within each session into daily practice. Homework helps clients to become their own therapist, reduces the potential for dependency on you and is the arena for weakening their irrational beliefs and strengthening their rational beliefs. Homework tasks can be cognitive (reading and/or writing), behavioural (such as staying in an aversive situation until the client's disturbed thoughts and feelings diminish), emotive (for example, forceful self-dialogues between the client's irrational and rational voices), and imaginal (mentally rehearsing new behaviours). Burns reports 'a strong positive correlation between compliance with these self-help assignments and therapeutic improvement' (1989: 545).

Homework is a vital component of REBT and homework assignments should be negotiated at the end of every session (including the first one). Some clients might wonder why their verbal reports of changes in their irrational thinking are not sufficient proof of progress. We would answer that behavioural evidence gained from homework tasks is the best form of verification of cognitive change. Homework can be seen as the unexciting side of therapy, the slog between sessions. The client's role then is to see the link between homework and achieving his goals: carrying out the agreed homework tasks, discussing with you what he has learnt from them, increasingly taking the lead in designing these tasks, and realising that homework is the route towards becoming an independent problem-solver.

Understanding and overcoming resistance to change

Client resistance is likely to occur at some stage in therapy and it is important for the client 'to understand what resistance is and what you [the client] can do about it so as not to let it undermine both what you've already accomplished and what you can further accomplish.' (Grieger, 1991: 49). Ellis (1985, 2002) suggests some reasons for client resistance which include:

• fear of the discomfort of change;
• fear of disclosing 'shameful' thoughts, feelings and actions;
• feeling hopeless about the possibility of change;
• fear of subsequent failure following initial success;
• following a hidden agenda instead of working towards the agreed goal.

What your client can do about tackling his resistance is to identify, challenge and change the irrational beliefs engendering it (for example, 'I must be certain that if I make progress I will not then slip back. To do so would be awful') in order for progress to continue (say, accepting that some slippage might occur but that it does not remove or erode the progress already made).

Learning to tolerate the uncertainty and unnaturalness of the change process

Some clients might believe that change is a smooth, uneventful and comfortable process. A successful therapeutic outcome cannot be guaranteed, nor that expenditure of effort will not be wasted (though you can probably guarantee the client that his problems will not improve unless he starts to tackle them). Tolerating uncertainty means not demanding 'I must see improvement straightaway'; improvement – or lack of it – can be detected through regular progress reviews.

As clients begin to change by strengthening their conviction in their new rational beliefs and weakening their conviction in their old irrational beliefs, some of them might complain of feeling 'unnatural' or 'strange' (for example, 'I don't feel I'm me any more'). This phenomenon is often referred to as 'cognitive-emotive dissonance' (Grieger & Boyd, 1980) and is an internal conflict between new and old ways of thinking, feeling and behaving. Such dissonant reactions are to be expected. As we remind our clients: 'If it ain't strange, then it ain't change.' Cognitive-emotive dissonant states need to be tolerated but they will eventually pass.

Clients who tell themselves 'I can't stand feeling like this' will prolong this phase of the change process or terminate therapy prematurely. For example, a client who stopped drinking after years of heavy consumption eventually relapsed as he would not persist in tolerating the 'strange and disorientating sensations' of being sober. Telling himself repeatedly and forcefully that these sensations were to be expected and coped with, would have been more helpful to him in adapting constructively to the removal of alcohol from his life.

Becoming a self-therapist

The ultimate aim of REBT is for clients to become their own therapists – this aim is usually discussed from the first session onwards. If your client does not make use of the REBT skills in his own life after formal therapy has ended, then he will tend not to sustain any of the changes he has made in therapy. The essence of self-help in REBT is the deliberate use of REBT skills in the client's own life. It follows from this that a major part of your job as an REBT therapist is to help your client acquire such skills, and for the client to apply himself diligently to learning these skills. At the earliest opportunity in therapy, the client needs to take more responsibility for the running of each session and the direction of therapy: setting the agenda, putting his problems within the ABCDE model of emotional disturbance and change, suggesting and designing homework tasks, revising goals if necessary, putting forward dates for termination, etc.).

If some clients baulk at becoming a self-therapist, remind them you will not always be there to prompt them to take action and offer encouragement – they need to become self-prompters and self-encouragers, hence the vital role of homework tasks in this process of becoming increasingly self-reliant as a problem-solver. This discussion concentrates your client's mind on the need to take personal responsibility for solving his problems and taking charge of his life in a way that promotes happiness and minimises unhappiness. Being a self-therapist means both present and future emotional problem-solving – a lifelong commitment to the principles and practice of REBT (of course, your client does not have to make this commitment).

Learning about and implementing relapse prevention

Once your client has made progress in tackling his problems, he might believe that this is the end of the story of his difficulties and termination of therapy is the next step (e.g., 'Things are going all right for me, so everything seems okay'). However, before this step is taken, relapse prevention measures need to be discussed, that is, looking at areas of continuing vulnerability in his thinking and life, and developing coping plans to deal with these vulnerabilities. Point out to the client that relapse prevention is not based on pessimism regarding his future progress, but the likely progress of a fallible (imperfect) human being. A relapse-prevention strategy can help prevent a client's lapse (a partial return to a problem state) turning into a relapse (a full return to a problem state).

We encourage clients not to disturb themselves about the prospect of a lapse or relapse but, if it does occur, to focus on identifying the factors leading up to it, distilling constructive lessons they can learn from it and continuing to work towards the goal that the lapse or relapse interrupted. Therefore, your client needs to integrate into his new rational outlook the fact that he is still a fallible human being who will almost inevitably experience a lapse or relapse (possibly more than once), and that hard work is still required of him to reduce the adverse impact of the cognitive and behavioural vulnerabilities that make him prone to experiencing further episodes of emotional disturbance.

Focusing on maintaining therapeutic gains

While relapse prevention looks ahead to potential problems the client might encounter, maintenance of therapeutic gains requires the client to consider what he is going to do on a daily or regular basis to prevent or minimise backsliding (returning to old patterns of thinking, feeling and behaving). The client might believe that his therapy gains will be self-perpetuating but you can ask if him physical hygiene looks after itself: 'Will you remain clean and fresh if you don't wash?' In a similar way, his mental hygiene needs frequent attention, such as reminding himself why self-acceptance provides an enduring basis for emotional stability rather than self-esteem, and acting in ways that continue to support his gains, perhaps entering situations where he might be rejected or criticised.

Your client can see himself as the guardian of his new rational philosophy and thereby look for ways to maintain and strengthen it, while being aware of and seeking to reduce further the lingering influence on him of his old irrational beliefs.

In the next chapter, we will discuss how to help clients to tackle the self-generated obstacles that hinder their therapeutic progress.

It is sometimes said that the path to true love never runs smooth. Well, it is also true that the path to psychotherapeutic change rarely runs smooth and there is a plethora of possible obstacles for clients to negotiate if they are to achieve and maintain such change. Two major books have been devoted to this subject as it pertains to REBT (Ellis, 1985, 2002; Neenan & Dryden, 1996) and interested readers are encouraged to consult these sources. We will confine ourselves here to discussing some of the major obstacles within the client that are manifested in the process of REBT and how therapists can address these effectively during the course of therapy.

Your client believes that change is not possible

Some clients come to REBT quite discouraged about the possibility of achieving psychotherapeutic change. We are not referring to clients who are depressed and are sceptical about achieving anything meaningful from REBT because of their depressed mood. Rather, we are referring to a more enduring, less mood-driven idea that these clients hold, that for them change is just not possible. Such clients may have had previous experience of being unsuccessful in therapy and come to REBT as a last and, in their view, doomed attempt to gain some help.

Unless this obstacle is identified and dealt with, you will waste much effort because your client's pessimistic view of the possibility of change means that he will only engage superficially in the process of REBT, or not engage at all. In both cases, you have the sense that you are working very hard and your client is hardly working at all.

In dealing with the 'I can't change' obstacle it is important that you do not attempt to persuade the client of the falsity of this notion using general arguments since such attempts are rarely successful. Instead, we suggest the following strategies. First, if your client's pessimistic view of the possibility of psychotherapeutic change stems largely from previous unsuccessful attempts at therapy, then it is important that you stress how REBT differs from these other approaches and how your client can effect change by using a variety of techniques designed to help him overcome his problems. Second, we suggest that you discover if your client has ever had the experience of personal change even though at the time he was sure he couldn't change. If he has, this provides you with an opening to encourage your client to at least consider the possibility that the same thing may happen again in REBT. If your client has not had this experience, then we suggest that you ask him if he is prepared to try REBT with an open mind while not constantly rehearsing his 'I can't change' idea. If he is prepared to engage in REBT with an open mind, he often finds that he can experience some degree of personal change, and when this happens you can use this as evidence against your client's 'I can't change' idea.

Your client opts for short-term 'solutions' to his problem

REBT basically outlines a long-term solution to client's problems. As described throughout this book, this basically involves helping your clients to identify, challenge and change the irrational beliefs that underpin their problems, and consistently encouraging them to think and act in ways that strengthen their conviction in their developing rational beliefs. As discussed in Chapter 2, belief change is the preferred form of therapeutic change, but as we have also mentioned there are other forms of psychotherapeutic change. REBT therapists are flexible, and if they cannot encourage clients to change their beliefs, they will urge them to make as constructive a change as possible.

Before coming to therapy, it is likely that your clients will have tried to solve their problems in a number of ways which may have brought them short-term relief, but these 'solutions' do not, in fact, solve their problems, but often unwittingly perpetuate them. One of the main tasks that you have in helping clients overcome their obstacles to change is to discourage them from using these short-term 'solutions' to their problems. A brief outline of such 'solutions' and how best to tackle them follows.

Denial

Some clients try to help themselves deal with their emotional disturbance in the short term by denying (to themselves and/or others) that they have problems. This, of course, becomes manifest at the very beginning of therapy and needs a prompt response. The best response is an empathic, non-pressurising one where you encourage your client to reflect without shame on his present situation and, if necessary, to imagine that a loved one was in his situation and to consider what he would advise his loved one. Would he encourage this person to admit to her problems and commit herself to the helping process or would he encourage her to say that she did not have problems. By contrast, pressurising the person to admit to his problems is usually counterproductive.

Denial is also fuelled by shame. If you are ashamed of something then one way of dealing with it is to deny that it is a problem for you. Addressing the shame-fuelled self-depreciation helps the person admit to you – and perhaps even to himself – that he has a problem.

Over-compensation

Some clients attempt to deal with their problems in the short term by over-compensating for them, adopting a stance that is the very opposite to how they truly feel. Doing so helps them to feel good in the very short term, but only serves to reinforce the irrational beliefs for which they are over-compensating. A common form of over-compensation is the adoption of a superior stance to cope with feelings of inferiority. In helping a client to refrain from adopting an over-compensatory position and to deal with the irrational beliefs that underpin his problem you need to help him to:

1   Understand the function of his over-compensatory stance and the irrational beliefs that it is meant to keep at bay.
2   Construct alternative rational beliefs and a more functional behavioural and thinking alternative to the over-compensatory stance which he currently adopts.
3   See that the new rational beliefs and the more functional stance help him achieve his goals and that, by contrast, the irrational beliefs and over-compensatory stance only serve to perpetuate his problem.
4   Choose which path he wishes to take (rational beliefs + non-compensatory stance vs. irrational beliefs + over-compensatory stance).
5   Tolerate the short-term discomfort that will ensue when he chooses the former path over the latter.
6   Adopt the non-compensatory stance repeatedly, while rehearsing the rational beliefs that are consistent with it.

Safety-seeking behaviour

Safety-seeking behaviour is overt or covert behaviour that the person performs to keep himself (from his point of view) safe from threat in the short-term. Thus, a woman who is scared of fainting in a supermarket may hold on to her friend to prevent herself from fainting. Safety-seeking behaviour has a similar function to over-compensatory behaviour and has similar poor long-term results. Consequently, a therapeutic approach similar to the one outlined above with respect to over-compensatory behaviour is called for, with one addition: it is important for the client to test out the validity of her cognitive consequence at C. Thus, at some point the woman above needs to let go of her friend to see whether or not she faints.

Behaviour change not in line with cognitive change

Behaviour that stems from irrational beliefs can easily become habitual and your client may perform such behaviour even though he has challenged and begun to change his irrational beliefs. If this happens with your client, we suggest that you:

1 Help him understand this phenomenon.
2 Help him identify a functional alternative to this behaviour.
3 Explain that there is a difference between experiencing an urge to enact the habitual, but dysfunctional behaviour (action tendency), and acting on this urge.
4 Encourage him to monitor and accept the existence of his urge to enact the dysfunctional behaviour.
5 Help him see clearly that he has a choice. He can either act on this urge or act against this urge by enacting the functional alternative behaviour.
6 Help him understand that doing the latter is far less familiar than the former, and if he chooses the latter he will experience the acute discomfort of acting unnaturally.
7 Help him see that doing this is in his best long-term interests and that he needs to remind himself of this fact when he is making the choice at point 5.
8 Help him see that this discomfort lessens as he becomes more used to acting functionally.

Your client has reservations about his goals

We mentioned earlier on that it is important that you help your client to establish goals for change (p. 36). Doing so gives both you and your client a direction for therapy and ensures that both of you are working together for the best interests of your client. We pointed out in that discussion that there are three types of goals that are linked together: emotional goals, behavioural goals and cognitive goals. We showed that with a client who is anxious about asking women to dance and avoids doing so, his emotional goal would be to feel concerned rather than anxious about being turned down; his behavioural goal would be to ask women out rather than avoid doing so; and his cognitive goal would be to recognise that, of a number of women that he asks to dance, some will dance with him and others will not, rather than thinking that nobody will dance with him.

You might think that setting these goals is straightforward and that clients will be clearly committed to goals that are so clearly healthier for them than their currently experienced problems. Often this is the case, but not always. For, sometimes, your client may have reservations about the goals you have elicited from him and this becomes apparent when you notice that your client is making less progress towards his elicited goals than you might realistically expect.

There are two major occasions when it is useful to check for the possible existence of client reservations about elicited goals. The first occasion is at the point when you elicit these goals from your client. Asking questions such as: 'What negative consequences, if any, might you encounter if you achieve your goals?'; 'What would you lose, if anything, if you were to achieve your goals?'; 'Do you anticipate any problems working towards your goals?' helps to stimulate your client's thinking on this issue. Some REBT therapists advocate that clients carry out a more formal cost–benefit analysis on their problems and goals in order to assess fully their clients' reservations about their goals and the process of working towards these goals. A typical cost–benefit analysis form asks a client to list both the advantages/benefits and the disadvantages/costs of a) his problem and, separately, b) his goal, from both a short-term and a long-term perspective and as experienced by himself and relevant others. The information that you get from this form often alerts you to potential future reservations that the client may have about his goal if none is currently apparent.

The second major occasion to check whether or not your client has reservations about his goals is when it becomes clear that he is not working towards them as diligently as might be expected. Of course, there may be many reasons why your client may not be working towards his goals other than goal-related reservations, some of which we will discuss later in this section. When you suspect that your client is encountering an obstacle to change, then you should, at the very least, consider that this may be due to his reservations about his stated goals and it is worth reviewing your client's goals with him, as well as any reservations that he might have about them. In this respect, it is important to note that clients' goals do change over time and, consequently, not to expect that the goals you elicited from your client at the beginning of therapy will remain unchanged throughout the process of REBT.

Your client has reservations about rational beliefs

In dealing with client problems, one of your major tasks as an REBT therapist is to help your client achieve his goals by encouraging him to identify and challenge his irrational beliefs and change them to their healthy rational equivalents. In doing so, it is important that you help your client see that his rational beliefs can help him achieve his goals. Unless your client sees this, he may not be motivated to acquire these rational beliefs. However, assuming that you have successfully helped him to see this rational belief–goals connection, you may still encounter client resistance to change because he may have reservations about adopting the rational beliefs. Here are some typical client reservations about non-dogmatic preferences, non-awfulising beliefs, high frustration tolerance beliefs and self- and other-acceptance beliefs and how to deal with these reservations when you uncover them in therapy.

Non-dogmatic preferences lead to decreased motivation to reach goals and to lesser effort

Your client considers that 'musts' both enhance motivation and lead to increased effort and, by contrast, sees non-dogmatic preferences as diluting motivation to achieve prized goals and as leading to lesser effort. For example, one of your clients may argue that adopting the non-dogmatic preference: 'I want to do well in my forthcoming examination, but I don't have to do so' would mean that he wouldn't study as hard as he would if he had kept his demand: 'I must do well in my forthcoming examination.' Since the client wants to study hard, he is likely to resist adopting this rational belief as long as he sees it interfering with his motivation to study and the effort that he would put in while studying.

Response: You need to help your client understand that non-dogmatic preferences do not preclude strong motivation and determined effort to achieve valued objectives. It is true, for example, that your client's demand may lead him to study hard for his exam, but his study may well be punctuated with increased anxiety and task-irrelevant thinking that will probably interfere with the efficiency of his studying. In this respect, your client's demand may also prevent him from taking healthy breaks from studying and lead him to become overly tired – a state which is conducive neither to good study habits nor to optimal examination performance. By contrast, your client's non-dogmatic preference will increase the efficiency of his studying by helping him focus on the content of what he is revising rather than on the task-irrelevant thoughts that stem from his demand, and will encourage him to take breaks from study which will help him stay fresh for the examination itself.

Anti-awfulising beliefs minimise the badness of very aversive negative events

Your client considers that an awfulising belief accurately describes the full aversive nature of the very negative event about which he is disturbed, and views the alternative anti-awfulising belief as minimising the badness of this event. For example, a client might argue that adopting the anti-awfulising belief: 'It would be very bad if my wife were to leave me, but it wouldn't be the end of the world' would mean viewing this event as slightly bad or moderately bad. As a result, he resists adopting this idea.

Response: You need to help your client see that adopting anti-awfulising beliefs does not preclude him from seeing personal tragedies as personal tragedies and catastrophes as catastrophes. A recent advertisement for an insurance company used the slogan: 'We won't make a drama out of a crisis.' The implication here was that the company would still respond to the crisis. REBT has a similar message for clients: it effectively urges clients to take the horror out of a crisis, but still to view the event as a crisis and to respond to it as such. So, in responding to your client who thinks that the above-mentioned anti-awfulising belief minimises the badness of his wife leaving him, you can point out that this would be a tragedy for him but, like other people, he could learn to transcend this personal tragedy, which he could not do if his wife leaving him were truly awful. For once you define something as awful, you are implying that you cannot transcend the experience, no matter how you think about it. In pointing this out to your client, it is important to keep stressing that it would be a personal tragedy for him if his wife were to leave him. In doing so, you are neither minimising nor exaggerating the badness of such an event. Rather, you are acknowledging that it is what it is: a personal tragedy.

Anti-awfulising beliefs condone others' bad behaviour

Your client considers that an anti-awfulising belief condones the bad behaviour of another person whereas the awfulising belief does not condone it. So, one of your clients might argue that adopting the anti-awfulising belief: 'It was very bad that my father left the family when I was young, but it was not the end of the world' would mean that he would be condoning his behaviour. Therefore, he resists adopting this rational belief.

Response: In rebutting this reservation, it is important to help your client to see the important difference between condoning something and holding an anti-awfulising belief about it. To condone another's bad behaviour means to absolve or to excuse the person for his behaviour. This is not done when one adheres to an anti-awfulising belief about this behaviour. Doing so involves holding the other fully responsible for his behaviour, asserting that it was very bad for him to act that way, while contradicting the idea that it is the end of the world that he acted very poorly. Thus, it is important to show your client that it was very bad, but not awful for his father to leave his family when he did and that he needs to be held to account for his behaviour and that understanding why he did it is not tantamount to absolving him of this responsibility.

High frustration tolerance beliefs discourage you from changing negative events

Your client considers that being encouraged to tolerate negative events means that he should grin and bear it, that he should take no action to change such events. Thus, your client might argue that the high frustration tolerance (HFT) belief 'It is hard to tolerate being criticised unfairly, but I can tolerate it' means that he should just put up with unfair criticism without doing anything about it. As such, he would resist adopting this belief.

Response: Here, help your client to see that far from leading to resignation, a high frustration tolerance belief helps him to change effectively a negative event by encouraging him to think clearly and objectively about how he can best respond to the negative event in focus. By contrast, the alternative low frustration tolerance (LFT) belief leads to impulsive, non-reflective behaviour which decreases the chances that your client will respond effectively to the negative event. Thus, it is important to show your client that developing a tolerance of criticism enables him to think about how to answer the unfair criticism and thus respond effectively to the person making it. It does not mean suffering in silence in the face of such criticism, nor does it mean lashing out at the other person (a response more characteristic of an LFT belief).

Self-acceptance beliefs encourage resignation or complacency

Here your client thinks that the term 'acceptance' either means that you have to resign yourself to the way that you are and that change is not possible, or it encourages complacency in that although change is possible there is no need to change because you are OK the way you are. As a consequence, your client resists your efforts to encourage him to accept himself.

Response: It is important that you explain to your client exactly what self-acceptance means from an REBT perspective: acknowledging that you are a complex being comprised of many different aspects (positive, negative and neutral). Thus, it is certainly possible for you to accept the whole of you and still recognise that there are negative aspects of yourself that can be changed. Thus, self-acceptance does not mean self-resignation nor does it encourage complacency. Indeed, because an attitude of self-acceptance minimises psychological disturbance, this attitude promotes change because it enables the client to divert his energies from focusing on what he doesn't like about himself, to understanding the factors that are involved with such aspects and also to intervening productively on these factors. Lack of self-acceptance leads to disturbed feelings and so diverts the client's energies away from constructive self-change.

Your client thinks that insight is enough

Many people believe that when you understand the factors that account for the existence of psychological problems – and what you need to do to deal with these factors – this insight leads to psychotherapeutic change. If only this was the case! If your client holds to this view, then you need to explain the difference between intellectual insight and emotional insight. From an REBT perspective, when your client has intellectual insight he has a cognitive understanding:

- that irrational beliefs underpin his psychological problems;
- that the alternatives to these irrational beliefs are rational beliefs, and that holding rational beliefs represents the most stable way of overcoming his problems;
- that he needs to question his irrational beliefs and see that they are false, illogical and have largely dysfunctional consequences;
- that he needs to question his rational beliefs and see that they are true, logical and have largely functional consequences;
- that he needs to question both sets of beliefs many times before he begins to truly believe his rational beliefs and disbelieve his irrational beliefs;
- that he needs to act and think in ways that are consistent with his developing rational beliefs and do so repeatedly, while facing relevant critical As;
- that while facing these As he needs to refrain from acting and thinking in ways that are consistent with the irrational beliefs that he wishes to disbelieve.

Intellectual insight can be gained from books and does not lead to enduring psychotherapeutic change because it does not involve your client *doing* anything to change. Thus, when your client has intellectual insight he may understand, for example, that demanding that his boss like him is irrational, but he still has the dysfunctional effects of holding this belief and he may further understand that believing that he does not need his boss to like him is rational, but he does not realise the true emotive, behavioural and thinking benefits of this rational belief.

Emotional insight, on the other hand, can only be gained by putting intellectual insight into practice and by doing so regularly and with commitment and energy. This form of insight cannot be derived from books. In short, if your client believes that intellectual insight is sufficient to promote psychotherapeutic change, it is important to disabuse him of this idea. Emotional insight involves 'blood, sweat and tears' and can only be gained from the gymnasium of experience. Intellectual insight, by contrast, can be gained in one's armchair without breaking sweat.

Your client doesn't understand the concept of self-help

The noted rational psychiatrist, Dr Maxie C. Maultsby, once said that the effectiveness of therapy depends on the extent to which clients use the therapy with themselves. In this respect, good therapy is essentially self-therapy. If your client does not understand this and thinks that therapy only really occurs in the consulting room and when dispensed by the therapist, this poses a significant obstacle to client psychotherapeutic change. So, it is important that you review with your client your respective responsibilities in the therapeutic process (see Chapter 3 for the client's responsibilities). When this obstacle to psychotherapeutic change is based on ignorance alone, discussing with your client his responsibilities in REBT is all that is required.

Your client isn't prepared to work for change

More frequently, it is the case that your client understands the concept of self-help, but isn't prepared to act on it. There may be a number of reasons for this refusal to work for change. The following three reasons are typical.

'I don't have the time to carry out self-help assignments'

Your client may have a very busy lifestyle that may or may not reflect his psychological problems. The last thing such clients want is more work and they may very well baulk at the idea of carrying out self-help assignments because they see these assignments as adding to their considerable burden. When your client's very busy lifestyle is the consequence of his irrational beliefs, you may have to postpone encouraging him to carry out self-help assignments until he understands this and you have helped him in therapy sessions to challenge and change these irrational beliefs and to develop rational alternatives to these beliefs. You can then introduce the idea of giving up activities – a behavioural plan that is consistent with his rational beliefs – and encourage him to do this so that he can strengthen these rational beliefs. Once he has done this he will be more accepting of the idea of carrying out self-help assignments that can be introduced as 'work designed to encourage him to work less hard'.

If your client's busy lifestyle is not the consequence of his irrational beliefs, but reflects realistic economic pressures, this poses a different problem. In this case, we suggest that you encourage your client to do self-help assignments at spare moments, such as while having breakfast or while on train journeys to and from work. I (WD) usually state that because of my other commitments, I do not write in large blocks of time, but in 10-minute periods here and there. It is amazing how much you can get done if you utilise small periods of time.

'I shouldn't have to carry out self-help assignments'

Some clients who have narcissistic tendencies understand in general that change comes about through one's own efforts, but hold that they should be the exception to this rule. As one of my (WD) clients once said to me: 'I'm paying you good money for this therapy, you should do my homework assignments for me!' The idea that the therapist does homework assignments for the client and the client gains the benefit from the therapist's work is an interesting one and if ever a therapist devises such a scheme that therapist will soon be very rich indeed!

In reality, of course, your client will only reap therapeutically what he is prepared to sow in terms of doing self-help assignments. Therefore it is important that you challenge your client's idea that he shouldn't have to do homework assignments. The best way to do this with clients with narcissistic traits is to use behavioural experiments rather than cognitive arguments. First, tell your client that he may be correct in assuming that he may benefit from REBT without doing homework assignments and ask if he is prepared to be open-minded in putting this idea to the test. Clients, in general, do not respond well to being told that they are wrong and this is particularly the case with narcissistic clients. If your client agrees to put this idea to the test, suggest that for an agreed period he will not do self-help assignments, and for the same period he will agree to do such assignments, at the end of which he will evaluate the results of the experiment. If your client conducts the experiment properly he will usually conclude that he derived more benefit from doing self-help assignments than from not doing them. It is particularly important that your client arrives at this conclusion himself if he is to change his view that he shouldn't have to carry out homework assignments.

'I'm too lazy'

Some clients refuse to carry out self-help assignments because they claim to be too lazy to do anything to help themselves. This self-description, of course, demonstrates a philosophy of low frustration tolerance and clients who describe themselves as such have problems underpinned by the same philosophy. They literally bring this philosophy to therapy. The way to deal with this major client obstacle to change is threefold. Firstly, it is important to encourage your client to dis-identify with their so-called 'laziness'. Help him to see that he is not a lazy person, but holds a set of beliefs that lead to him not being prepared to take constructive action on his own behalf. Such dis-identification encourages your client to see that he does not have to change his identity to help himself overcome his problems, only some of his beliefs. Secondly, suggest your client can use the issue of doing self-help assignments to address his LFT beliefs. If he agrees, you can help him challenge his LFT beliefs in traditional REBT fashion. In doing this we suggest that you lay particular emphasis on pragmatic disputing of LFT beliefs, encouraging your client to see that it is worth tolerating the discomfort of carrying out self-help assignment because they help him achieve his goals. Thirdly, help your client understand that when he holds an LFT belief about doing a self-help assignment, he predicts that doing the assignment will be far more uncomfortable than if he holds a high frustration tolerance (HFT) belief about doing the same assignment.

Having overestimated the discomfort he will experience, your client will avoid doing the assignment. After you have helped your client understand this dynamic, encourage him to conduct a behavioural experiment where he first undertakes to carry out a self-help assignment while holding an LFT belief and then doing one while holding an HFT belief. This should help him see that he constructs greater discomfort in his mind than exists in reality.

Your client is intolerant of the discomfort and unfamiliarity of change

A particular set of LFT beliefs constitutes a frequently encountered client obstacle to psychotherapeutic change. The object of this set of beliefs is change itself; sometimes it is the discomfort that your client experiences when he begins to change and at other times it is the sense of unfamiliarity that change brings. When your client begins to change, he will feel uncomfortable since this is an inevitable feature of psychotherapeutic change. If your client believes that he must not experience this discomfort then he will stop working to achieve his goals and will likely stop changing. In such a case, it is important that you help your client to see that:

- Discomfort is an inevitable part of change.
- Change-related discomfort can be tolerated and if one keeps one's goals clearly in mind then it can be seen that such discomfort is worth tolerating in that it aids goal attainment.
- Holding an LFT belief about change-related discomfort leads to the prediction of greater discomfort than does holding an HFT belief about the same form of discomfort.
- Continuing to act and think in ways that are consistent with developing rational beliefs will lead to a decrease of change-related discomfort.

If your client acts on these four insights then he will be well on the way to overcoming this obstacle to psychotherapeutic change.

When your client begins to change, he will experience a sense of unfamiliarity. As I (WD) often say to my clients: 'If it ain't strange, it ain't change.' If your client believes that he can't bear this unfamiliarity then he will engineer things so that he returns to the uncomfortable, but familiar state of his problems. Helping your client deal with this obstacle is similar to helping him to deal with the obstacle of change-related discomfort. Thus, help your client to see that:

- Unfamiliarity is an inevitable part of change.
- A sense of change-related unfamiliarity can be tolerated and – if one keeps one's goals clearly in mind – it can be seen that such unfamiliarity is worth tolerating in that it aids goal attainment.

- Holding an LFT belief about a sense of change-related unfamiliarity leads to the prediction of a greater sense of unfamiliarity than does holding an HFT belief about the same sense.
- Continuing to act and think in ways that are consistent with developing rational beliefs will lead to a decrease of change-related unfamiliarity and eventually a new sense of familiarity.

In this chapter we have discussed some of the major client obstacles to psychotherapeutic change and have given you some recommendations about how best to address these obstacles. In the next chapter we consider some of the obstacles to change that emanate from the therapist and suggest what you can do to address these obstacles.

In this chapter we look at how you block the client's progress by the irrational beliefs, unproductive ideas and behaviours to which you subscribe. Having regular supervision is essential in order to detect and change your irrational beliefs and counterproductive behaviours which could otherwise put a brake on your client's progress. In some cases, personal therapy may be indicated if some of your irrationalities persist, cannot be dealt with in supervision and are clearly detrimental to your clients' welfare.

You share the same irrational beliefs as your client

Paul Hauck (1966) called this issue 'the neurotic agreement in psychotherapy'. For example, one of your clients believes that without a partner she is worthless. Without explicitly agreeing with her, you internally 'nod' in agreement, perhaps thinking, 'She's hit the nail on the head.' When it is not clear if you subscribe to the neurotic agreement, look for clues that your normally competent practice of REBT is faltering: you may subtly change the subject when your client discusses material that you find very unsettling or you may be tentative – in contrast to your usual vigour – in disputing your client's irrational beliefs. Occasionally, when you share your client's irrational beliefs, you may attack these beliefs too vigorously. This can be a form of projection, or you may even hate yourself for holding such beliefs and thereby hate the client for reminding you of your own unacceptable irrationality. We will now outline two ways in which you can identify neurotic agreements in psychotherapy.

1 Pay attention to your disturbed feelings such as anxiety or anger, or look for signs that you may be ashamed of having such feelings: you may find yourself engaging in various defensive manoeuvres to protect yourself from experiencing these feelings, such as encouraging your client to look for solutions to problems instead of dwelling on painful issues (the longer he dwells on them, the more disturbed you will make yourself).

2   Listen to audiotapes of your therapy sessions when you suspect the presence of a neurotic agreement. Here, pay particular attention to your behaviour which may be defensive in nature. Once you recognise such defensive behaviour, it is easier to ask yourself what you are defending yourself against. Since doing this for yourself may be difficult, ensure that you are in regular supervision with a competent REBT supervisor who is likely to spot your 'backing away' from or avoidance of discussing particular client issues (for example, 'When your client keeps returning to this issue of being worthless without a partner, you either go uncharacteristically quiet or offer bland reassurance that she will find someone soon. What prevents you from getting to grips with her problem?').

Once you have identified a neurotic agreement and have accepted yourself for having an irrational belief which is similar or identical to that of your client, then use your REBT disputing skills on yourself: 'I certainly want a partner but there is no reason why I must have one. Without one, I can still be reasonably happy and accept myself, not condemn myself.' You can then remove yourself from the 'neurotic agreement' and return your focus to where it belongs – helping the client to find rational solutions to his emotional problems.

Another neurotic agreement might be where you delay in 'getting down to business' because you enjoy the client's company and want to prolong it, particularly if you have had a string of difficult or 'uninteresting' clients. Your easygoing approach, and the client's fondness for chatting instead of concentrating on what he is in therapy for, produces a relationship based on short-range hedonism instead of a business-like approach to problem-solving. We would suggest that the more you are enjoying therapy, the less likely it is you are doing therapeutic work (though, of course, a mutual pleasure can be derived from problem-solving). So the paradox emerges that if your client starts to improve because a clinical focus has now been established, then the 'life' of the easygoing and enjoyable relationship is threatened. As a result, you collude with your client to avoid making therapy as effective an endeavour as it might otherwise be.

You need to remind yourself that therapy is based on collaborative hard work and effort to realise the client's goals, not on the creation of a convivial atmosphere. Therefore, you will need to help yourself, before helping your client, overcome the philosophy of low frustration tolerance implicit in this collusive short-range hedonism. Additionally, you do not have to have interesting clients to offset the uninteresting or difficult ones, or do not deserve some easy times in therapy as a break from continual problem-solving, combating resistance or dealing with the 'same old problems' every day. Each client you help helps you to learn something about yourself and improve your relationship-building and problem-solving skills. Looking for an easy time in therapy will teach you very little about becoming an effective therapist.

You believe you need your client's approval

With this belief in the forefront of your mind, you will probably: a) side-step confrontation with your client when it is clinically indicated (perhaps the client keeps insisting that he cannot tolerate criticism from his colleagues); b) avoid eliciting or discussing painful feelings in case he thinks you are 'insensitive'; c) provide continual reassurance or even flattery as he discusses his problems; and d) 'forget' to discuss homework assignments if your client does not seem interested in doing so. If you do incur your client's displeasure, you immediately seek ways to placate him: 'I think you may have misinterpreted what I said. I did not mean to cause you any offence' – rather than elicit the reasons for his displeasure. As Wessler and Wessler (1980) point out, the list of approval-seeking behaviour can go on and on, all interfering with or blocking your client's progress.

Approval needs indicate conditional self-acceptance: your worth depends on what others (in this case, your client) think of you. Approval-seeking can be summed up as: 'They think, therefore I am.' The antidote to approval-seeking is self-acceptance – acceptance is something we give to ourselves rather than given to us by others. With this outlook, you allow your client to make up his own mind about you without engaging in placatory and pleasing behaviour to influence his decision in your favour.

Modelling self-acceptance helps your client internalise this outlook if self-depreciation is part of his presenting problems. Practising self-acceptance means you do not tip-toe around sensitive issues – you approach them with tact and empathy – because you are no longer worried about incurring your client's displeasure: 'I'm here to do my professional best for my client, not protect my ego.' If the client does show you any displeasure, you then deal with it 'head on' in order to forestall or repair any ruptures to the therapeutic alliance (for example, 'I think it would be helpful for both of us if I can understand why you get angry when I ask you questions about your partner's infidelity').

You believe your worth depends on your client's progress

When you believe that your worth as a therapist and person is contingent upon your client's progress, you will see his improvement as confirmation for you, not only of your clinical competence, but also of your personal worth; and when his progress stalls or appears to dissipate, you will see yourself as clinically incompetent as well as personally inadequate. Not that the client knows it, but you have given him the power to determine your self-evaluation ('Your success makes me a success'). As Wessler and Wessler remark:

> It is often the need to be successful that leads to conceiving of the client as resistant and makes the therapist particularly susceptible to... power 'games'. ...It

is also likely to lead to the related idea 'He must improve' and anger when he does not. The anger can be countertherapeutic and sometimes leads to the vicious circle of anger, resistance, more anger, and so on. (1980: 169)

When you believe your worth as a therapist and person is contingent upon your client's progress, you may assume the client is making progress without eliciting detailed feedback (a nod of the head or a 'hmm' from him will suffice) or looking for evidence. Assuming progress where none may exist means you do not have to hear 'bad news' and engage in self-condemnation because of it.

Power games, anger at your client for lack of progress, thereby not 'making' you feel good, or conducting therapy devoid of any meaningful feedback are all a waste of valuable therapy time. Your personal worth is not contingent upon your client's improvement or anything else in life. Your clinical competence is improved through – among other activities – regular supervision; approval-seeking will only bring about a decline in your competence. If your client is not making progress, then a clinical review of the case is required to ascertain the reasons for it. This might uncover mistakes you are making but provides opportunities to correct them; also, client blocks to change can be pinpointed. You will experience failure with clients from time to time and exhibit some incompetence in certain areas of your clinical practice. It is important that you accept these facts of clinical life. Tying such failure and specific acts of incompetence to your overall clinical competence and self-worth may mean you are reluctant to end therapy when all the signs indicate it is time to do so. As Persons observes, 'the therapist may continue an unsuccessful treatment far beyond the point where termination will be for both patient and therapist anything other than a demoralizing, painful and bitter event' (1989: 209–10). To avoid such an outcome, undertake regular progress reviews in an objective and collaborative way and challenge and change your irrational beliefs that link your worth with the client's progress. With this new outlook, proving your worth, as a therapist and as a person, is no longer an item on the therapy agenda.

Your self-disclosure is inappropriate

You may assume that sharing with your client your experiences of a problem similar to his will automatically establish a therapeutic alliance. Moreover, your frequent personal revelations of past problems show in your mind a solidarity of suffering with your clients. You may even end up working on your own problems alongside those of your client. Therapists who use therapy for their own needs probably subscribe to a major irrational belief: 'Because I am a person in my own right, I must be able to enjoy myself during therapy sessions and to use these sessions to solve my personal problems as well as to help my clients' (Ellis, 1985). Needless to say, the more you are focused on your own problems, the less time you will spend on your client's.

We would make three points with this issue of self-disclosure. First, the only valid use of self-disclosure is if it helps your client and this is determined through feedback: in what specific ways has your client found it helpful in understanding his own problems? If it has no clinical relevance for him, then stop using it. Second, self-disclosure should be used judiciously, not incontinently, otherwise your client 'suffers' from overexposure to your personal experiences. Third, your job is to provide therapy, not receive it. A client who attends for therapy to work on his own problems should not have to cope with yours as well. If your problems keep surfacing in therapy with your client, then you might need to consider therapy for yourself.

Arguing with your clients

When reasoned debate breaks down, arguing takes over. You may be trying to convince your client that, for example, he does have some irrational beliefs when he keeps denying it, that prolonged anxiety is an unhealthy negative emotion when he insists that it motivates him, or that he has to carry out his homework tasks when he cannot be bothered to. Arguing can quickly develop into a power struggle with winners and losers – whose views will prevail? When you argue with your clients, you usually put your ego on the line; therefore, you have to win in order to avoid seeing yourself as the loser – an incompetent or weak therapist. Becoming angry over your client's reluctance to see things your way means you are acting as a poor role model for handling conflict constructively. As well as wasting valuable therapy time, arguing creates a tense milieu that is hardly conducive to promoting therapeutic change.

To stop arguing, stop demanding that your client must see things your way – let him make up his own mind. Encourage him to voice his objections to or reservations about REBT. He is more likely to see the sense in your viewpoint by your display of open-mindedness and the quality of the arguments you present, not through trying to force him into agreement. Therefore, leave your ego outside the counselling room. Go through an entire session without trying to convince your client of anything and see what happens (Walen et al., 1992). Ask your client, for example, what he would regard as an irrational belief or what he understands by the word 'irrational'; what are the costs of prolonged anxiety, not just its supposed benefits; and what are the likely consequences for therapeutic change if he does not carry out his homework assignments? Following these points, reasoned debate can then make a reappearance within a genuinely therapeutic milieu.

Lecturing too much

REBT therapists are encouraged to adopt the role of an authoritative, but not authoritarian, teacher (Ellis, 1978). The teaching you will provide is an emotional education within the ABCDE model of emotional disturbance and change. Being overly didactic means the client does little introspective work as you provide the answers for him, and consequently he becomes a passive participant in therapy, waiting to be spoon-fed with information.

Your client is unlikely to recall, and thereby retain, this information outside of therapy as he has not processed it in his own words. You may believe that a great deal of lecturing and telling will inevitably result in the client both gaining insight into his problems and taking constructive action to tackle them. However, information overload or didactic battering can leave your client feeling overwhelmed and he consequently 'switches off' or drifts away to find a pleasant mental experience.

We would suggest that you let your client's brain take more of the strain in therapy, that is, encourage him to think things through for himself. In this way, he can find a solution to his problems that is owned by him, not imposed or given by you through constant instruction. Only do so much lecturing, and then only in bite-sized chunks, to stimulate your client's thought processes. Socratic dialogue suggests a collaborative relationship, excessive lecturing indicates a dependent one.

You are passive in therapy

Instead of being too didactic, you may behave in a passive way (perhaps lots of 'hmms' or nods of the head) thereby militating against the active–directiveness of REBT. Being passive might mean you spend too much time listening to your client's interminable explanation of his presenting problem or allowing endless ventilation of his feelings. Questions are vague ('So what was happening for you in that situation?') instead of focused ('What were you telling yourself in that situation in order to make yourself so angry?') and confrontation is avoided as you believe this would impair or destroy the supportive nature of your interactions with your client. Instead of the client following you in order to learn REBT, you follow the client, which is likely to result in REBT being taught in a haphazard and unsystematic way.

The active–directiveness of REBT is based on the assumption that it is more effective and faster in helping clients to change than a passive or non-directive style of therapy. You are required to be active in, for example, asking focused questions, collecting assessment data, limiting the introduction of extraneous material, curbing client rambling or verbosity, problem-defining, goal-setting, teaching the ABC model, disputing irrational beliefs, and negotiating homework tasks – all these and other activities are aimed at directing clients to the cognitive core (rigid musts and shoulds and their extreme derivatives) of their emotional and behavioural problems. In order to help your client move from problem assessment to goal achievement, you can see yourself 'as a kind of herd dog who guides the patient through an open field of distractions, keeping the patient on course' (Walen et al., 1992: 229).

Listening in REBT is active, not passive: you are listening for the ABC components of your client's problem, not just to the problem itself. Confrontation in REBT is assertive, not abrasive, and points out the discrepancies between your client's thoughts, feelings and behaviour – discrepancies the client might not be aware of if you do not bring them to his attention. REBT advocates that clients develop robustness in tackling their problems and this viewpoint is unlikely to be communicated to your clients if you continue to adopt a passive stance.

Putting words in your client's mouth

REBT hypothesises that rigid and extreme beliefs underlie emotional disturbance (for example, a client feels ashamed because he believes, 'I absolutely should not have lost my temper with my colleague but, as I did, this shows everyone how unstable and weak I am'). Offering hypotheses to your clients is an important part of REBT practice as it encourages them to disconfirm these hypotheses ('No, I'm not demanding certainty of outcome. I may be demanding something about the outcome but I'm not sure what it is'). Additionally, clients are also encouraged to put their disturbance-inducing into their own words rather than fit into an REBT formulation of such thinking ('No, I can't hear any musts in my thinking but I can hear, loud and clear, the word failure').

However, if you apply REBT theory unthinkingly, you will automatically assume that musturbatory beliefs (musts) will always be present in your client's thinking, and therefore not offer your hypotheses for disconfirmation or allow your client to phrase his irrational beliefs idiosyncratically. For example, 'What you're really saying is "I must not make mistakes" rather than "I don't want to make them." It's the must that drives your anxiety.' Putting words into your client's mouth also occurs with rational beliefs: 'So now you're feeling concerned, what you're telling yourself is, "I would prefer not to make mistakes, but there is no reason why I must not make them."'

Putting words into your client's mouth can lead to some of the following outcomes: you turn your client into a ventriloquist's dummy; you are perceived as arrogant for always knowing the right answer and being a mind-reader; your client develops a healthy resistance to being told how he is thinking; and you are practising lazy REBT, i.e. not fully explaining the REBT model of emotional disturbance: 'Let's get straight to the musts. Why waste time?'

If you teach the B–C connection clearly and vividly, the chances are your client will see for himself the link between his musturbatory thinking and his unhealthy negative emotions (if your client does not accept key tenets of REBT, then a referral to another therapist is suggested). However, some clients will continue to struggle to see this connection, so take time and be patient in carefully establishing it. When the words in your client's mouth belong to him, and are not put there by you, then REBT is much more likely to be a personally meaningful experience for him.

Your interpersonal style reinforces your client's problems or resistance

REBT suggests that different clients respond to different types of therapeutic bonds with their therapist; a one-size-fits-all approach means that some clients may drop out of therapy because they cannot 'fit' into your style. For example, one client wants a formal relationship with you while another client prefers a relaxed and informal approach; if your approach is always a formal one, then the latter client is likely to struggle to adapt to your style. Developing different and genuine interpersonal styles with your clients is acting like an 'authentic chameleon':

> The therapist makes use of the most helpful facets of his or her personality in order to establish rapport with a particular client. The goodness of fit is examined by seeing the therapist–client relationship on a continuum extending from a very close-knit, dependent bonding at the one end, to a rather formal, businesslike investment at the other. (Kwee & Lazarus, 1986: 333)

Interpersonal difficulties also arise when you pay little, if any attention, to your client's personality style. For example:

• Being too active–directive with a highly reactant client is likely to lead to a power struggle in therapy.
• Allowing a client with a sociotropic personality style to become dependent on you because you provide him with excessive warmth and nurturing.
• Increasing a client's passivity by always taking the lead in therapy and not encouraging the client to make more effort.
• Making sessions emotionally charged with a client who is over-excitable or has a histrionic personality style.
• Engaging an overly intellectual client in further intellectual discussion is likely to inhibit expression of his real feelings about adverse events in his life.

These examples are likely to result in an alliance that is counter-therapeutic as it hinders client learning and thereby entrenches maladaptive behaviour instead of fostering constructive changes in it.

To start forming a productive alliance, you can ask your client for his preferences regarding the type of bond he favours forming with you; give him a Life History Inventory (Lazarus & Lazarus, 1991) to complete, which includes asking clients to specify how therapists should ideally interact with their clients and what personal qualities they should possess; and elicit from clients any previous experiences of therapy with particular emphasis on the kind of bond that promoted therapeutic change.

As therapy progresses, you can seek regular feedback on your bond behaviour in order to make adjustments to it in the light of your client's comments (your client might ask you to tone down your humour and act more seriously). We are not suggesting that you automatically change your bond behaviour because, on occasions, to do so will reinforce your client's problems (for example, if your client wants lots of reassurance from you regarding his health anxiety, to comply with his request would help to maintain this anxiety).

Paying attention to your client's personality style will help you develop an interpersonal environment that maximises his opportunities for therapeutic learning. In other words, the relationship 'milieu' promotes – not inhibits – client learning. To return to the above examples of personality styles:

- Highly reactant clients value autonomy and freedom of choice, so ask them to do things instead of telling them, provide a lot of interpersonal freedom and present options to them which maintain their sense of self-direction and control in therapy. With these clients, 'it might be best to put them in charge of their own homework' (Dowd, 1996: 4).
- Encourage sociotropically orientated clients to test their fears of 'striking out alone' and becoming their own therapist by engaging in small experiments which will avoid them becoming dependent on you.
- With passive clients, encourage them to participate more in therapy, for example, 'It is important that I hear your views on your problems and what to do about them', so that their 'brains take more of the strain' of problem-solving.
- With overexcitable or histrionic clients, use a 'quieter' and calmer interpersonal style in order to reduce their emotional arousal to a level where they can adequately reflect on their experiences. This reflection is primarily accomplished with cognitive techniques in order for them to step back from their volatile feelings.
- With overly intellectual clients, use a more emotionally charged learning atmosphere. Dryden et al. suggest that you 'should preferably endeavour to inject a productive level of affect into the therapeutic

session and employ emotive techniques, self-disclosure and a good deal of humour' (1999: 284) to help these clients release their feelings.

The choice of which interpersonal style to employ should be based on clients' accounts of which factors produce the best learning environment for them. By developing a learning profile of each client, you can plan your therapeutic strategy and the techniques to implement this strategy. However, care needs to be taken that you do not use a mode of learning that may perpetuate your client's problems, such as cathartic or abreactive techniques with overexcitable clients.

Having unrealistic expectations of your clients

Because REBT seems simple to understand and apply through its ABCDE model, you might expect all of your clients to make rapid progress in tackling their problems. Therefore, you cover a lot of ground in the first and subsequent sessions, take client nods for understanding and acceptance of the points you have made, and set ambitious goals for change. While some clients will make rapid progress, others will struggle to keep up with you and feel overburdened with and confused by all the information you give them. For these clients, change is slower and they want more time to process information and discuss issues, but they may feel resentful at being hurried along by you.

REBT may seem simple to you (after all, you have trained in this approach) but it is new to your clients, so eliciting feedback from them will tell you how much progress they are actually making and what pace they want in therapy. We suggest that you slow down and allow your clients time for 'digesting' – discussion and absorption of information presented by you. Create a milieu in which 'thinking things over' is given sufficient time and attention (Neenan & Dryden, 2002). By doing this, you are more likely to have clients responding positively to REBT rather than showing resentment towards you.

Another unrealistic expectation you may hold is that all intellectually bright and articulate clients will automatically respond to REBT because of its emphasis on disputing irrational beliefs through rational thinking. You may take for granted that your client understands the differences between rational and irrational thinking and can quickly grasp REBT concepts. Because of these assumptions, you may see feedback largely as a waste of time ('Let's cut to the chase. The client's got the brainpower for it') and believe the client's progress is self-evident rather than established through the collection of evidence.

Your expectations will not apply in every client case; there will be exceptions. As Wessler & Wessler point out:

If my rule is (we will assume its validity) '90 percent of bright, verbally sophisticated clients readily understand the concepts of REBT,' the question still is 'Is my client sitting here one of the 90 percent or one of the 10 percent?' I had better check it out, for in the individual case, given that or any other rule, I am either 100 percent right or 100 percent wrong. (1980: 171–2)

What you expect and what you get can be very different, so 'check it out' in every case to avoid therapy being driven by your unvalidated assumptions, whatever they are.

Disturbing yourself about your clients' disturbances

While concern and compassion are important qualities to display to your clients as they relate their problems to you, being too concerned and desperate to 'heal the client's pain' can lead you to be just as disturbed as your clients. For example, you could make yourself depressed about your client's misfortunes in life or get angry about how others have treated him. At this point, your clinical focus will be lost as your disturbance takes precedence over your client's; instead of one disturbed person in therapy, there are now two. Also, if you are still disturbed after your client has left your office, you will not be able to give your full attention to your next client.

We would suggest that your disturbance arises not from caring about your client's troubles, but caring *too* much about them: you believe you have to suffer because you see your client suffer. Caring too much about your clients is best handled if you accept

the rational idea that *one does not have to be disturbed over other people's problems and disturbances*. Get hold of that idea securely, think it through in great depth, and accept it as a wonderfully sane piece of advice. ... Stop pitying people and you will bring yourself back on the right track. (Hauck, 1980: 238–9; italics in original)

To avoid caring too much for your clients, ask yourself the following questions: 'How does my suffering alleviate my client's?' 'Am I more clinically effective when I am emotionally disturbed?' and 'Might I be showing, through my distress, that my client's problems are unbearable and insoluble?' If you want to help your clients overcome their disturbances, then start with your own.

Your goal is different from your client's

REBT literature frequently refers to encouraging clients to strive for profound philosophical change (giving up all rigid and extreme thinking), but the majority of clients we see are not interested in achieving this goal. Their aims are usually more modest, such as being less anxious in certain situations or coping better with low moods. Tension can develop in the therapeutic relationship or arguing can erupt when your client realises that his goals are being ignored in favour of yours. In your mind, you believe you are doing your best for your client because you can 'see' the patterns of disturbance-inducing thinking in his life which he currently cannot. Once he sees what you can see, then he will readily agree with your goal aims for him. However, the client is more likely to see himself as being forced to change in ways that he has not agreed to or cannot see the sense in.

The goal in REBT is chosen by the client, not by you. Discussion can take place if the goal is unrealistic, too vague or is likely to be countertherapeutic. This is legitimate goal negotiation. Clients can move through a number of stages of change if they choose to: situation-specific, cross-situational or pervasive (i.e., throughout their life). Clients are likely to set more ambitious goals for themselves if they feel in charge of the change process.

We would also like to add that agreeing on goals does not mean automatic agreement on the means to achieve these goals. For example, the agreed goal is for your client to feel concerned instead of anxious in fearful situations; he suggests distraction as the best method to achieve this goal, whereas you insist on exposure to his fears (e.g. 'Distraction is likely to perpetuate your fears'). Again, discussion is the best way forward, focusing on the short- and long-term advantages and disadvantages of your respective change methods. As an experiment, the client can try dealing with his fears in his own way before trying it your way and then he can compare the results of each technique.

Being judgemental about your clients

REBT therapists can be forthright with their clients ('What prevents you from getting to the sessions on time?' 'How will arguing with everything I say help you overcome your problems?') but should do their best to avoid being judgemental ('Poor timekeeping is a sign of a poor character'; 'You really are an argumentative bastard, aren't you?'). If you are judgemental, you are not showing respect towards your client or accepting him as a unique individual, and you are impairing the development of a relationship that should be built on trust in order to allow your client to talk freely about himself and his problems. Your client may see you as always critical of him as he can never meet your standards of 'correct' behaviour.

Your judgemental attitude may reflect your intolerance of your client's weaknesses ('I can't abide a self-pitier') or your LFT-related impatience ('When are you going to start working in therapy instead of whining all the time?'). If your client already sees himself as a bad person, your judgemental attitude towards him will only reinforce this self-image.

If you are being judgemental about some of your clients, are you aware of it? Even if you are, regular supervision of your audiotaped sessions with a competent REBT supervisor is important in order to detect and help change your judgemental tendencies. When you detect your judgemental attitudes, accept yourself for having them but work hard to remove them ('Despising my client for being a self-pitier will teach me nothing about helping him. Therefore, I will focus on the problem, not morally judge the person'). Making clinical judgements helps you decide on the best course of treatment for your client, making moral ones is based on whether you think your client deserves to be helped by you and will receive your best efforts.

Accepting your client as a unique, unrateable and fallible human being does not mean you also accept his behaviour when it has breached guidelines for acceptable conduct in therapy (if, say, he is frequently verbally abusive towards you). The reasons for your client's behaviour can be examined, but the behaviour itself has to stop if he wants to prevent the session – even therapy – terminating prematurely. In this example, you are making a specific, not general, judgement about a specific behaviour of your client, and stressing the implications for therapy if no change in that behaviour is forthcoming.

Believing you have to challenge your client's irrational beliefs immediately

REBT does have a 'let's get on with it' approach to emotional problem-solving but it also recognises that clients need time to settle in to therapy. However, you might be tempted to dispense with this 'settling in' period and start disputing the first irrational belief uttered by your client. In your zeal to 'get on with it' and prove what a competent REBT therapist you are, your client is likely to feel bewildered and under attack ('Why doesn't she listen to me instead of shooting me down all the time?'). The client may then show active or passive resistance to your 'quick on the trigger' style of REBT with you then trying to 'crush' your client's resistance with even more vigorous disputing. Needless to say, this interpersonal conflict hardly bodes well for the development of a productive therapeutic alliance.

 Immediate disputing of irrational beliefs is not usually a sign of a proficient REBT therapist but of a hasty and ill-prepared one. Care needs to be taken in constructing a therapeutic alliance, socialising clients into REBT, gathering background information, assessing clients' presenting problems, gaining feedback, pinpointing the clinically relevant irrational beliefs to challenge rather than the first ones that appear – once these activities have been completed, it is then much more likely that your clients will be in the right frame of mind to engage in disputing. Setting the stage for disputing rather than headlong rushing into it will help to create the impression of clinical competence and thereby reduce the chances of client resistance occurring.

You believe that your clients should be as hard working and responsible as you are, should listen to you carefully, and should always push themselves to change (Ellis, 1985; 2002)

While some clients undoubtedly will want to work hard in therapy (even harder than you in some cases), others definitely will not, for a variety of reasons. For example, to make this demand on

> alcoholics and substance abusers is to practically guarantee emotional dysfunction. You then insist that clients be free of part of their major constellation of problems – namely, low frustration tolerance and rebellion – that are often the heart of their addiction. … Blaming these clients for the attitudes and habits that define their addiction is clearly countertherapeutic. (Ellis et al., 1988: 142).

Condemning and rejecting such clients for being unmotivated, difficult and resistant leaves them in no doubt as to how harshly judgemental you are and may reinforce their own self-condemning beliefs (for example, 'He looks down on me like everyone else does. I suppose I am no good'). When these clients drop out of therapy, as they are likely to, you may conclude sagely: 'They are not ready to change.'

If your client is unmotivated, it is your job to uncover these blocks to change and help him overcome them, not condemn him for the very problems for which he is seeking help. If you have to put more work into therapy than he does, so be it. There is no rule in therapy (except in your head) that effort has to be divided equally. If you show your client that you are working hard for him because you believe in him, he may start to work hard on his own behalf and take responsibility for changing his self-defeating attitudes and habits.

Failing to persist in helping your client to bring about change in his life

You might be pleasantly surprised how quickly your client agrees with the REBT view of the development, maintenance and amelioration of emotional disturbance ('It does make sense. In fact, it's amazing how true it is when I think about it'). Both you and your client feel optimistic that therapy will proceed in a relatively straightforward and uneventful fashion. However, this early optimism can fade as translating REBT theory into daily practice becomes more difficult than anticipated and your client starts to question REBT in a more critical way ('I'm not sure now how true REBT really is because there are some things that I could not accept myself for doing, or if my partner left me and I lost my job then it would be awful').

As the client's progress bogs down and he forgets, distorts or continues to find fault with rational beliefs, your low frustration beliefs are triggered ('I can't stand going over the same points every week! When the hell is it going to sink in?'). What you envisaged as relatively easy brief therapy has, from your viewpoint, turned into really effortful brain-wearying torture. Your impatient and brusque manner is clearly evident to your client and he now becomes wary about telling you of his difficulties with understanding and/or implementing REBT. You do not want to hear the 'usual complaints' and he is reluctant to voice them.

Understanding rational beliefs is not a one-off event even if your client seems to initially grasp the points you are making. You will need to repeat your interventions, perhaps many times, within the framework of high frustration tolerance ('Even though it may be a boring grind, I can stand going over the same points every week until my client understands and acts on them'). Introduce variety into repetition to avoid making it a 'boring grind'. For example, some clients will respond favourably to rational beliefs being taught through the use of films, literature, or contemporary or historical figures. Accept yourself for holding low frustration tolerance beliefs, apologise to your client for your behaviour stemming from them and then return your clinical focus to helping your client, not disturbing yourself: 'Now which aspects of REBT do you find difficult to understand or agree with?'

In the next chapter, we look at the interplay between therapist and client factors that produces ruptures and impasses in the therapeutic alliance.

In this chapter, we discuss the confluence of client–therapist factors that hinder the former's progress. We propose that by opening a channel of communication to discuss these factors, you and your client will be able to stand back from, observe and comment upon the unfolding interaction in therapy. Through this process, impasses to change can be removed and alliance ruptures repaired.

When your client believes that he has no freedom of choice

You might believe that pointing out to your client that he has freedom of choice will encourage him to see the possibilities of thinking, feeling and behaving differently with regard to his current problems. However, your client may vehemently deny that he has any choice in how he responds to adverse events in his life: 'You don't understand. If I really had the power of choice, do you think I would choose to be depressed? To be so upset over my partner leaving me and all the other problems I have?' You may then respond that every situation contains choice, that we have control over our actions and feelings, not events or others, and that not acknowledging that we have a choice is itself a choice. This may sound like a clever reply but it is likely to reinforce the client's sense of failure in not being able to deal effectively with his problems.

Your emphasis on freedom of choice can sound to your client as a variation on the 'you could pull yourself together if you wanted to' advice he gets from others. The client believes you do not understand how the world looks through his eyes, while you believe he is deliberately refusing to take responsibility for his problems and frustrating you in your attempts to help him. As Safran and Muran observe:

> The fact that one is currently feeling self-critical prevents one from fully seeing the way in which one is currently choosing to live one's life in a self-defeating way. To experience oneself as choosing one's unfortunate life is a painful thing. A person in pain and distress is already full of self-loathing. He is feeling

blamed for something over which he feels he has no control. It thus becomes extremely hard for him to acknowledge the way in which he may be contributing to his own problems. He has a constant experience of trying and yet failing and then feeling condemned by self and others for his failure. He thus experiences the will as atrophied. He has no experience of choosing his actions. (2000: 83)

Your client may withdraw further into himself in therapy and your belief that you are unable to help him deepens. An impasse ensues.

The first step in breaking this deadlock is to understand your client's internal reality – why he believes he has no control over anything in his life – and then help him to stand back from his subjective reality in order to determine if it is an accurate or distorted view of events in his life. Glover (1988) suggests that a major reason why clients feel so helpless is that they are too focused on changing the general context of their problems and pay scant attention to what they actually contribute to the problem and what they can change, namely, their behaviour. If your client develops an awareness that choices are made moment-by-moment or at the point of action, then this can help him regain a sense of self-direction and responsibility for the choices he makes. So help your client understand that he is making choices as therapy unfolds. For example:

- Your client engages in 'yes, but …' replies to your questions. You can point out that 'yes' signals assent to change, a choice, while the 'but', another choice, opts to maintain the status quo in the client's life.
- Your client says he has no willpower to effect meaningful change in his life but, paradoxically, shows a quiet determination to see no merit in anything you suggest to bring about such change. He is exercising choice through the application of 'won't-power', an oppositional role in therapy (Neenan & Dryden, 2002).
- Putting items for discussion on the session agenda or saying 'I don't know what to talk about' shows personal agency at work. In the latter case, your client has decided at that moment not to think about what he wants to discuss.
- Even though your client says he is always unsure whether to come to the next session, he still chooses to do so. His decision militates against the idea that he is helpless to decide anything for himself.

While helping your client see that choice does inform his actions in therapy, it is very important that this is said in a positive and supportive way, not in a condemning or accusatory 'catching the client out' tone of voice such as, 'Why do you keep denying what is clearly evident: you do have choices? Why can't you admit it?' By offering your client unconditional acceptance as a fallible and suffering human being, he may then be able to internalise compassionate self-acceptance and thereby acknowledge the self-defeating and problem-perpetuating nature of some of his actions, both in and out of therapy. As your client realises that he does have some influence over how he feels and behaves, this renewed sense of personal responsibility has two important consequences: 'First, it puts you back in charge of that which you *do* potentially have control over; and second, it reduces futile efforts to control the uncontrollable, and enables you to accept rather than worry (or feel guilty) about negative events that occur in spite of your contribution [to them]' (Glover, 1988: 109; emphasis in original).

When your client believes that validation of his distress is the purpose of therapy

When your client first attends therapy, it is to be expected that he will talk at some length about his problems and ventilate his feelings about them (perhaps he is angry and ashamed about being in an abusive relationship). You will show empathy, warmth, acceptance and respect towards your client, as well as develop a cognitive conceptualisation of his presenting problems, and this will form the basis of your treatment plan. You may believe that, through your empathic communication with the client, he is now ready to think about what is required of him in terms of problem-solving. However, your client may have little interest in problem-solving or thinking about change. As Leahy points out,

> Some patients may view the entire function of therapy as ventilation and validation. From this perspective, the therapeutic session should consist of the patient ventilating his complaints and emotions and the therapist reflecting back to the patient how awful life is for the patient. Simply 'being understood' becomes the goal of therapy … this ventilation–validation model may result in the persistence of the 'victim script' in therapy: the patient repeatedly focuses on how his or her life is really difficult, and the therapist becomes an audience and supporter for this view. (2001: 61)

Paradoxically, the more your client feels understood by you, the less able he will be to solve his problems – validation without victory we might say. As an active–directive REBT therapist, you will probably be getting restless at being an 'audience and supporter' of your client's endless ventilation and want to move into action mode, identifying, challenging and changing your client's irrational beliefs. You keep reminding your client that the goal of REBT is emotional problem-solving, but he increasingly feels that he and his problems are being invalidated by your indecent haste to achieve this goal: 'Only when you truly understand what I'm going through, will you be able to help me. I don't feel convinced at the present time that you really do understand me.' You may wonder at this point if a referral to a non-directive therapist is called for or you may grit your teeth and hope that in the next session or two your client will signal that he now feels understood by you and is ready to move on. We would suggest that with any impasse in therapy, you need to establish and maintain a channel of communication between you and your client which deals with metatherapy issues, concerning matters relating to therapy itself (Golden & Dryden, 1986). Activities that occur within this channel of communication can be seen as involving negotiations and renegotiations about therapeutic issues. Using the channel to deal with this particular impasse, you can point out that you will never be able to 'truly understand' what your client is going through, for the simple reason that you have not lived his life or experienced his experiences. You are, therefore an outsider struggling to understand the distress he feels and why he believes it is so hard for him to change. You can only ever achieve a partial understanding of his problems.

Given your unalterable empathic limitations, does your client think a partial understanding has been achieved and can he 'live with that' in therapy? (If your client says that partial understanding has not been achieved, what criteria is he using to determine when it has?) I (MN) once saw a client who had been a prisoner of war during the Korean War. He repeatedly told me how terrible his suffering had been and I kept telling him I completely understood what he went through because I had read books and seen documentaries on the war. He kept shaking his head and saying in an angry voice, 'You don't understand. How could you? You weren't even born when I was captured.' Only when I admitted my empathic limitations and stopped uttering standard therapist clichés, did he say, 'Now we're getting somewhere' in tackling his depression.

Another issue to resolve with the client is that ventilation is likely to strengthen his emotional disturbance:

> The venting of feelings is a highly cognitive activity in which irrational ideas that give rise to strong emotional reactions are rehashed. Giving vent to feelings thus serves to further habitate the ideas that cause the disturbance so that, in effect, the client actually practices being disturbed. As a result, s/he gets worse rather than better. (Grieger and Boyd, 1980: 118)

Your client may feel temporarily better as he 'gets things off his chest' but these 'things' are likely to stay 'on his chest' as he repeats the same disturbance-inducing ideas in each session. Weaning the client off endless ventilation can start with an agreement to spend some time in each session first engaging in ventilation and then developing rational responses to his irrational ideas: 'If you really want to feel differently, then you need to think and behave differently, otherwise you will remain emotionally stuck.' In this way, therapy begins to move in the direction of the client becoming a self-therapist and away from perceiving himself as a victim who is powerless to change anything in his life.

You can also focus on the limitations of validation as an end in itself. What will be the impact on the client's life if he leaves therapy feeling validated but the problem is still intact? To overcome this limitation, first establish that your client believes he has been understood by you, then ask your client what he has understood from his experiences that he can carry forward in his life. Leahy calls this process recognising the loss but learning the lesson, part of his 'dialectic of validation and change' (2001: 81). For example, a client who was dismissed by a company to which 'I gave my all' is still angry and hurt about how unfairly he was treated but, in considering what he has learnt from his experiences, he says that he will 'keep something in reserve for myself as I want a life outside of work', and that no matter how hard he works, there is no law of the universe or workplace that states he must be treated fairly.

While REBT literature suggests that you get your client beyond the ventilation stage as quickly as possible, it is not always easy to do this. If you give the impression that listening to your client's 'awfulising' accounts of his unhappy life is something you have to endure before you get to the interesting (disputing) part of therapy, do not expect much – if any – therapeutic movement from him. However, if you find truth in the client's viewpoint, he is likely to find truth in yours (Leahy, 2001). In this context, it is important to validate the tragic aspects of a client's experience without confirming his awfulising belief about these aspects. This mutual 'truth seeing' helps to facilitate the emergence of hope in the client and the beginning of therapeutic movement for both of you.

When you do not like your client

Your expressed ideal might be to like every client you deal with but, in reality, there will probably be a few clients you encounter whom you do not like, such as those who express racist or sexist views, have an unremittingly cynical outlook or lead a lifestyle you do not approve of. Your dislike of your client can show itself in many verbal and non-verbal ways which communicate to him that you are having trouble tolerating his presence in the same room as you; sometimes you may deliberately engineer arguments with him and let him know that his views are unacceptable to you. You may hope that he will not return to therapy and thereby solve your problem for you – having to help someone you do not want to help. If he stays in therapy, you might make some small effort at problemsolving (trying to remember that you are supposed to be a counsellor) but a lot of your mental life in the session will be focused on what you dislike about him. Therapy is not about giving your clients a thumbs up or down depending on their opinions, outlook or lifestyle. If you cannot work with clients whose views you dislike,

> then counselling is in grave danger of appearing ridiculously self-indulgent and overly precious. If counselling is to be seen as a service for those in psychological distress, then it has to operate as such. It cannot cocoon itself against a world that contains much that many of us dislike. (Walker, 1993: 79)

You are not there to reform your client's character or change his values so they reflect yours. If he expresses views you disagree with (say, racist or sexist views), you can tell him you are opposed to such views and, if clinically relevant, you can examine why he holds such views. For example, a white client I (MN) saw said that since being mugged by two black men he could not trust any black person. I asked him if he would be unable to trust any white person if he had been mugged by two white men. He replied 'no' but would consider if his lack of trust was already evident before the attack and intensified by it. If his views are not clinically relevant, then do not allow yourself to get sucked into debating them: 'Your views on women and ethnic minorities do not help me to understand your problem, how it is being maintained or how to overcome it. Let's stick to what is on the agenda.'

If you do not like your client, Ellis suggests that therapists

> can accept themselves and their negative attitudes and may thus be able to focus on suitable helpful procedures and thereby surmount this handicap. In using RE[B]T I can almost always focus so well on my clients' problems, and especially on showing them how to correct their Bs and other thinking errors, that it hardly matters that I personally do not like some of them and would never select them as my friends. (1985: 26)

You may not be able to 'focus so well' and distract yourself from your personal dislike of your client, so we suggest you try to find something about the client that you do like even if it is only that he turns up on time. This may help you to see that your client has many aspects, not all of them unpleasant (from your viewpoint). Your dislike of him is not the whole story of his life – for example, what good things has he done that you know nothing about? Keep asking yourself if you are treating this client differently from a client you liked: 'When he doesn't do his homework, I give him a hard time. If I liked the client, I would focus on what we could learn from not doing the homework', and bring all these issues to supervision for discussion.

If your client asks if you like him, we recommend that you give a balanced but honest answer such as: 'I struggle to like you because I often focus on your views, not on your problems, and that gets in the way of giving you my professional best. My job is to help you, not judge you.' Your client may say he does not like you ('You're a patronising git. You think you know it all just because you're a bloody counsellor!'). To what extent does your client's dislike of you prevent him from being receptive to your suggestions for tackling his psychological distress? Discussing your mutual dislike of each other can clear the air and, in our experience, lead to the formation of a productive working alliance ('If we get sidetracked again by what we dislike about each other, let's step back from therapy, sort it out and then get started again. Okay?').

If you cannot temper your dislike for your client and this undermines your attempts to help him, then a referral to another therapist is in order (the same applies to your client's dislike of you). One final thought. Doctors, nurses, social workers, paramedics, and dentists are required to help people irrespective of their feelings towards them. There is nothing unique or special about your role as a therapist that allows or requires you to select whom you will work with.

Not dealing constructively with your client's transference reactions

Some clients may react to you as they do to significant others in their life. For example, a client with a dependent personality may want you to tell him what to do and thereby remain passive in therapy in the same way as he behaves with others outside of therapy. You may adopt the role of an authoritarian therapist as you think it will help your client ('Don't worry. I'll solve your problems for you'), or enjoy the role because you can feel omniscient and omnipotent and get a lot of satisfaction from the client's worshipful attitude towards you. Though your client may carry out your 'orders' to please you, your relationship is not based on collaboration and helping him to develop more independence in his life. The more he appears to change, the more he actually stays the same.

Whether you adopt or enjoy the role of an authoritarian therapist, remember it hinders your client's progress – he is likely to become dependent on you instead of developing autonomy. As Beck et al. observe:

> These patients do, at least initially, need some active guidance and practical suggestions by the therapist in order to become engaged in the treatment. A totally nondirective approach could be too anxiety-provoking for these patients to tolerate for long. However, when the patient asks the therapist to tell him or her what to do, the therapist needs to be careful to use Socratic questioning and guided discovery, and help the patient arrive at his or her own solutions. (1990: 292)

You can help your client to stand back from his transference reaction and elicit the beliefs maintaining it (for example, 'I must not lose the approval of others and, therefore, I have to be subservient to get it'; 'I can't bear to make decisions on my own'), and examine the costs of subscribing to such beliefs (such as the need for approval, lack of self-confidence, fear of being abandoned or rejected, or being crushed by criticism). You can use the relationship as a 'schema laboratory' (Padesky & Greenberger, 1995) to help your client develop autonomy-related beliefs ('I can make decisions for myself'; 'I can learn to be self-accepting in the face of others' criticism or rejection of me').

Collaboration will not be equally divided at the beginning of therapy but more of the responsibility for guiding therapy and supplying its content should gradually pass to your client. Successfully completing small experiments both in and out of therapy (such as voicing his opinions to you and engaging in activities when on his own) indicate your client is starting to take control of his life as he becomes more independent in his relations with others.

When your countertransference issues interfere with helping your client

Countertransference refers to the thoughts and feelings you have towards your clients – for example, your heart-sink reaction to one client, 'He's right in what he says – everything is hopeless'; and your increasing anxiety about the imminent arrival of another, 'She just argues against everything I say. She'll make me feel useless.' When examining your countertransference, you need to become your own therapist. In the first example, you may have allowed yourself to be 'sucked into' your client's sense of hopelessness by agreeing with his belief that he must see immediate improvement in order to feel hopeful about ameliorating his depression. By returning to your role as an empathic but detached observer of his problems, you can point out that seeing light at the end of the tunnel will take more time and effort, or that light has already been glimpsed but the client discounts the improvement that has occurred, such as, 'Improvement means to me that I can go back to work tomorrow, not just being able to wash my car.'

In the second example, if your client argues against everything you propose to help her, this does not prove your 'uselessness' as a therapist, but that you probably have a difficult client to deal with. Instead of dwelling on your uselessness, make yourself useful by asking your client to suggest a problem-solving plan that she could argue in favour of: 'It is easy to shoot down another person's suggestions, but harder to suggest something yourself that you will support and act on. Any ideas?' Problem-solving is a collaborative endeavour, so ensure that your client is pulling her weight in therapy.

No therapist is immune to experiencing countertransference. Ellis (2001) provides an example of enjoying a client's company so much that he avoided challenging her low frustration tolerance (LFT) beliefs because he succumbed to his own LFT, namely his fear that if he confronted her, she might leave therapy. Once Ellis realised how his own countertransference was interfering in his work with his client, he tackled his own LFT as well as hers.

Leahy proposes 'that the countertransference is an excellent window into the interpersonal world of the patient' (2001: 6) as it can be used constructively to understand the adverse impact your client may have on others in his life besides yourself. For example, if you feel impatient and speak curtly to your client because 'he never stops bloody complaining', your reaction may well reflect how others in his life react to him (the client says that 'the phone and the doorbell don't ring much these days. I suppose no one wants to talk to me'). Your countertransference reaction may reflect the reactions of others: 'Since the client is probably behaving toward you as to other people, you are in a good position to give feedback that others may not be willing to disclose; that is, how his or her behaviour influences you' (Walen et al., 1992: 246).

Thus, you may say that you feel irritated and frustrated by the client's non-stop complaining (give examples) and these feelings interfere with your efforts to help him. Could his behaviour be the reason for his increasing social isolation: 'What do you think is the likely reaction of your friends and colleagues to your continual complaining?' Your client may not appreciate this kind of feedback but, nevertheless, admits there is some truth in it. This admission can then be used by your client to consider what changes he could make in his interpersonal world that might help him to reverse his social isolation.

When your client keeps probing into your personal life

Though it is to be expected that some clients will ask you personal questions such as 'Are you married?' or 'Do you have children?', there might be a client who is very inquisitive about your personal life. You might answer a few of his questions to satisfy his curiosity but more questions are forthcoming and the focus of therapy seems to be on you instead of your client. You might become defensive and ask irritably: 'Why do you want to know so much about me? You're the one who wanted to come to therapy.' The client might reply: 'I'm not going to reveal intimate secrets about myself to a complete stranger', or 'I'm just trying to find out if you practise what you preach.' At this point, therapy might develop into a tennis match with each of you trying to return the session focus to the other person.

In order to resolve this stand-off, we suggest that you give a brief biography of your training and qualifications or a few examples of practising what you preach, such as learning self-acceptance or high frustration tolerance, and then ask your client what he has gained from this information and how he sees you now. This might do the trick and your client may now be ready to talk about himself because he sees that you have a 'human face, not an impersonal mask'.

On the other hand, your client might use this information against you, perhaps saying, 'How can you help me, if you've had similar problems to me? I thought therapists were supposed to avoid these sorts of things.' The client may have put you on a pedestal, but now realises you have feet of clay. You can point out that the notion of an infallible therapist is a myth and, therefore, looking for one will be fruitless, but clinical competency in problem-solving is another issue. You are a competent therapist who can help your client if is he willing to commit himself to engaging collaboratively in several sessions of therapy and then holding a progress review.

It may transpire that your client has a pattern of idealising would-be helpers, then rejecting them once he finds flaws in their character. You can help your client discover what is maintaining this pattern ('I've got this belief that only a special kind of person can help me'), and how to halt it by reconceptualising his notions of specialness ('There is no super-special person, but we are all special in our own way. The therapist is a special person who can probably help me if I give him the chance').

When a mutual attraction develops in therapy

As Ellis (1985) observes, if your client is attracted to you it does not necessarily involve a transference reaction but, more straightforwardly, that you have the qualities he finds highly desirable in a woman. Because he does find you attractive, he may impede his own progress (by not carrying out his homework tasks or holding back from discussing his problems in detail) in order to prolong his stay in therapy. He may dress inappropriately for therapy (but not if he was going to a party or night-club), ask whether you are single or attached, what qualities you find desirable in a man and how you would, hypothetically, deal with a client who was attracted to you. You may enjoy the attention you receive from him, take particular interest in your dress and appearance on the day of his appointment, let the sessions overrun and allow therapy to stray into exploring non-therapeutic issues (say, what you both like doing in your spare time). Your meeting with your client is more of a date than a session of therapy.

This impasse (though it may not feel like one to you or your client) can be difficult to deal with as it requires the 'spell' of attraction to be broken and proper therapy to commence by helping the client to deal with his presenting problems. It is your responsibility to bring therapy back on track. If you reflect on your behaviour in the session and bring it up in supervision (which might require some shame-attacking on your part), you will realise how countertherapeutic your behaviour is. You can explain this to your client: 'I certainly find you attractive and would have enjoyed your company if I had met you outside of therapy. However, I met you in therapy and our relationship can and will only be a professional one. I forgot this fact for several sessions and, therefore, was not focused on helping you. I regret my behaviour and will now put it right.'

Elicit feedback from your client in response to your behavioural change. The client might feel hurt over your rejection, disappointed that the 'fun' has stopped and there is no chance of having a romantic relationship with you, or angry that you were 'leading me on'. Whatever your client's reaction, your point will be inescapable: therapy is not the place to find romantic or sexual fulfilment. Encourage your client to identify, challenge and change any irrational beliefs that prevent him from accepting this fact, such as 'As I am attracted to my therapist, I must continue in therapy indefinitely. I can't bear not seeing her.'

When your client's attention is eventually focused on the 'mundane' tasks of problem-solving and he accepts there is no possibility of developing a non-professional relationship with you, he may start to talk about his problems in detail as he sees there is no benefit now in withholding information in order to prolong his stay in therapy.

When your client's 'know nothingness' leads to tension and frustration in the relationship

That clients will reply 'I don't know' to some of your questions is to be expected. However, when a client says it repeatedly and without any obvious effort to process your questions, you may see this as recalcitrant behaviour, or as the client playing games with you. Your frustration with your client's 'know nothingness' may boil over into anger with you making demands on your client accompanied by mind-reading: 'You must know the answer. You know that you know the answer. Why did you come to therapy if you're not prepared to answer my questions? You play games in the park, not in therapy.' Your demands for information and your client's seeming inability to provide it maintains a mutual state of ignorance about the latter's problems (interestingly, in supervision you might echo your client's 'I don't knows' to your supervisor's suggestions to repair this rupture in the alliance and 'open up' your client's thinking).

We would suggest that instead of asking further questions about your client's problems, let the 'I don't know' become the focus of clinical attention. What factors hinder your client answering your questions: lack of interest in or knowledge about them, not being prepared to expend mental effort to search for answers? How would the client feel if he could answer your questions? Are your questions too difficult to understand, are there too many too quickly, or do they seem irrelevant? 'I don't know' may be a protective response, with the client holding back from committing himself to change or exploring painful issues.

When I (MN) discussed these issues with a client who spent almost the entire first session saying 'I don't know' to virtually everything I asked her, two key LFT-related reasons emerged: first, the client was not prepared to struggle mentally to find answers if they were not immediately available to her; and second, she was reluctant to tolerate the emotional discomfort involved in exploring her current problems. When we looked at a cost–benefit analysis of continuing to subscribe to this 'double dose' of LFT, her conclusion was that the costs far outweighed any perceived benefits. Her 'I don't know' became 'I want to know more about my problem and what to do about it.' When she did say 'I don't know' to a question of mine, this was now based on genuine difficulty in answering the question, not a reflexive response to fend me off and protect herself from following my unwelcome line of clinical inquiry.

When your client compares you unfavourably with his previous therapist and you become resentful towards both your client and his therapist

It is a usual procedure in REBT to ask your clients about their previous experiences in therapy, both helpful and unhelpful, in order to use this information to construct a productive therapeutic alliance. However, a client may continually refer to his previous therapist in glowing terms (for example, 'She was so wise, witty and perceptive') and comment that therapy with you is 'hard going' and, by implication, not as satisfying. Everything you say he compares with his 'wise and perceptive' previous therapist and finds your comments lacking in substance, insight or 'not really understanding me, who I am'.

You may feel growing resentment towards your client ('Why the hell didn't he stay in therapy if it was so good? It couldn't have been that good because he relapsed') and towards his previous therapist and start taking pot-shots at her (e.g. 'Did she think she could walk on water?'). Meanwhile, you desperately try to say something insightful that will be acknowledged as such by your client. Your client keeps looking back to his previous therapist and you struggle to make your mark with him.

As always, both parties should step back from the relationship to engage in what Safran and Muran call metacommunication:

> Metacommunication consists of an attempt to step outside of the relational cycle that is currently being enacted by treating it as the focus of collaborative exploration: that is, communicating *about* the transaction or implicit communication that is taking place. This can be thought of as a type of *mindfulness in action*. It is an attempt to bring ongoing awareness to bear on the interactive process as it unfolds. (2000: 108; italics in original)

You could start the metacommunication by saying that, from your viewpoint, therapy is stalled because you do not seem to 'measure up' to the client's previous therapist, that you are trying to prove you are smarter than she was which you realise is pointless, and you are feeling frustrated that your client's mind is not focused on learning REBT.

You have different things to offer, including a different style (active–directive) and theory of emotional disturbance and change. Metacommunication should not involve blaming each other, and each person should take responsibility for their contribution to the current impasse.

The client's contribution is acknowledging that he is trying to justify the enormous amount of time and money he spent on his previous therapy by putting the therapist on a pedestal. If he admits you are competent, or even as good as she was, this would call into question his judgement about the time and money he 'wasted' on his previous therapy. You can point out that no experience is truly wasted if the individual is prepared to extract learning from it. In this case, his belief that long-term problems require long-term therapy to resolve them can now be tested using a much briefer form of therapy, if he allows himself to be receptive to REBT. Then he can compare the effectiveness of both approaches. In this way, focusing on learning, not justifying 'waste', can help to dissolve the impasse.

In the next and final chapter, we look at the process of change in REBT by examining the beginning, middle and end stages of therapy.

In this final chapter we discuss treatment issues that are relevant to the beginning, middle and end stages of therapy. Dividing REBT counselling into stages is a somewhat artificial convention which we have chosen to use in order to provide structure for the material presented in this chapter. In reality, it is impossible to differentiate so clearly between these stages within the counselling process. For example, issues related to the therapeutic alliance will have importance throughout the course of REBT, and are not restricted to the beginning stage. The material that follows should be viewed with this caveat in mind.

The beginning stage

Establishing a therapeutic alliance

Bordin (1979) provides a useful framework for conceptualising the therapeutic alliance by breaking it down into three major components: bonds, goals and tasks. The bond refers to the nature and quality of the interpersonal relationship that exists between you and your client. Goals are the objectives clients want to achieve with your help. Tasks are the activities that you and your client undertake to achieve the client's goals.

Bonds

In order to promote a productive bond, REBT therapists will make enquiries regarding an interactional style that is suitable for each client, as long as it does not reinforce your client's existing problems (see Chapter 7). Asking your client what constitutes helpful and unhelpful therapist behaviour – particularly in the light of previous counselling experiences he may have had – can produce a productive 'fit' between you and your client (for example, the client might want straight answers to his questions rather than the defensiveness he experienced with a previous therapist). Additionally, it is important to create an optimal learning environment for your client based on your knowledge of their personality style (say, a subdued and reflective ambience for clients who are easily excitable and prone to histrionics).

REBT is characterised by an active–directive problem-solving style which some clients may react against as they prefer to see the therapist in a passive role. This difficulty can be dealt with by presenting a rationale for your active–directive style; if this approach fails, you might try gradually increasing your level of verbal activity over the course of the beginning stage of therapy or making interventions which are well-timed with sharply focused questions to promote B–C thinking (that is, the role of your client's irrational beliefs in largely determining his disturbed emotional reactions to events in his life).

REBT offers clients unconditional acceptance as fallible human beings. This means, in practice, that you refrain from responding to your clients in a judgemental, condemning fashion when they report acts that society would consider unethical or morally wrong, or when clients behave inconsiderately to you. When confronted with these things, you can respond to your client in a reasoned, matter-of-fact and objective manner. Your response can foster an air of trust and openness within therapy, and can indirectly convey to your clients that they do not have to condemn themselves for their 'bad' acts which, in turn, may encourage them to reveal problems related to guilt and/or shame. You will, if necessary, bring to clients' attention that their behaviour in therapy is unacceptable and has to stop (for example, sustained verbal abuse of you) but you are willing to explore the reasons for such behaviour.

Goals

Goals in REBT should be agreed, explicit and conform to SMART criteria (see Chapter 5). Emotional goals are tackled before practical goals, as emotional disturbance interferes with practical problem-solving. Your client may receive only half the benefit of REBT if your focus is solely on the emotional solution: 'Dealing with the emotional problem is necessary, but *not necessarily sufficient*: resolving emotional problems gets rid of emotional disturbance; dealing with *practical* problems leads to self-actualization and improvement in the patient's quality of life. Both are important' (Walen et al., 1992: 52; italics in original). For example, a client may be depressed (emotional problem) about being in debt (practical problem). Helping to overcome his depression does not automatically mean he will now be able to devise and initiate an action plan to reduce or eliminate his debt – he might need help from you to do this.

Clients are encouraged to generate a problem list with a realistic goal established for each problem. You and your client need to agree on which problem to tackle first – this is usually the client's most pressing problem. This agreement communicates to your client that you are sensitive to his priorities and that he is expected to be active in the problem-solving process.

There may be times when the client's choice of problem is problematic. Perhaps he chooses to work on his anxiety (primary problem) when he is preoccupied with his shameful feelings (meta-emotional problem) about experiencing anxiety. If you detect the presence of a meta-emotional problem, bring this to your client's attention and present a rationale for dealing with it first ('With the shame in the way, you are unlikely to give me or yourself your full attention or your best efforts to overcome your anxiety'). If your client insists on working on his primary problem first, then go along with this until such time as it becomes obvious to both of you that progress is stalled because of the destabilising effect of the meta-emotion.

In order to make effective use of each session, establish an agenda at the beginning of it; this can help to promote goal congruence on a per session basis. The items on an agenda typically are: reviewing your client's homework assignments, topics to be covered in the present session, negotiating new homework assignments, and eliciting client feedback about the session. An agenda structures the session by an agreement on what topics are to be covered and prevents or minimises the risk of either you or your client mentally wandering off in the session. An agenda is not meant to be a straitjacket, and agenda-setting can be suspended if your client reports suicidal feelings at the beginning of the session, for example, or if an issue arises in the session that seems important to focus on rather than wait to be placed on the next session's agenda.

Tasks

REBT is based on collaborative problem-solving and, to this end, both you and your client have tasks to carry out in therapy. Your task is essentially to teach the ABC model of emotional disturbance (see Chapter 1) and what your client needs to do to change (see Chapter 3), while your client's key task is to internalise this model as the basis for becoming his own therapist (see Chapter 6). You can make explicit your respective tasks by saying something like this: 'My job is to help you identify, challenge and change certain unhelpful ideas and beliefs that maintain your current emotional difficulties. Your job, if you accept the REBT model, is to carry out this process both within and between sessions.' You and your client's tasks do not remain static throughout the course of therapy as more of the responsibility for directing therapy, making progress and maintaining treatment gains will fall to your client. From the first session onwards, you should be looking for ways to orientate your clients towards understanding that REBT is a self-help therapy.

Teaching the ABC model

For your clients to profit from REBT, they need to learn the three main insights of REBT and how to address their problems through the ABC model. The three main insights of REBT are:

1   Human disturbance is largely determined by holding irrational beliefs. To paraphrase Epictetus, a Stoic philosopher from the first century AD, 'people are disturbed not by things, but by their rigid and extreme views of things'.
2   We remain disturbed in the present because we continually reindoctrinate or brainwash ourselves with these beliefs and act in ways that strengthen them.
3   The only enduring way to overcome our emotional disturbance is through persistent hard work and practice – to think, feel and act forcefully against our irrational beliefs.

These insights, particularly the last one which needs to be clarified by example or analogy, address the problem identified by Hanna namely that 'One of the fundamental mistakes made in psychotherapy and counseling is to assume that clients understand change processes. If they did, change might be accomplished much quicker and easier on a routine basis' (2002: 43). These three insights act as a summary of REBT and provide a lifelong guide to emotional and behavioural problem-solving.

Teaching the ABC model is usually done didactically rather than Socratically because in the latter approach your client may come to the realisation that 'What I'm telling myself makes me angry, not the situation', but 'what I'm telling myself' does not correspond with REBT's conception of irrational beliefs ('I don't like being frustrated by others' vs. 'I must not be frustrated by others'). Being didactic reduces the likelihood of your clients learning the wrong lessons about the ABC model. Always seek feedback from your clients to determine if they have understood and agree with the points you have made (understanding does not mean agreement).

You can use elaborate models to teach the ABCs of REBT (see the money and lateness examples in Dryden, 1995: 53–66), or more straightforward ones such as how two people react differently to the same situation because one person evaluates the situation rigidly (for example, 'I can't stand boring meetings!') while the other person evaluates it flexibly ('I can stand them, but I don't like them') (see Neenan & Dryden, 2001). Assess the verbal and intellectual abilities of each client to determine whether you will be presenting an elaborate or straightforward example to demonstrate the ABC model (even a seemingly straightforward example can appear complex to some clients, so it is incumbent upon you to be creative in teaching the belief–emotion link).

When you have elicited problems for discussion, avoid jumping from problem to problem within a counselling session. Remaining focused on one problem at a time, and covering the essential steps of the change sequence (see Chapter 3), is usually the best means for teaching your clients the elements of REBT.

By the end of the beginning stage of counselling, your clients should have learned the three main insights of REBT and had some initial experience in identifying and disputing the irrational beliefs that underpin their emotional problems. You will have also introduced your clients to the concept of homework assignments which will serve as an important, if not crucial, vehicle for facilitating client movement from intellectual to emotional insight into their problems.

Bibliotherapy assignments (which involve clients reading REBT self-help texts) given at an early point in counselling can often help clients to become accustomed to the idea of devoting time and effort to working on their problems between sessions.

Dealing with clients' doubts about REBT

Some clients may express doubts about the effectiveness of REBT in helping them resolve their emotional problems. In responding to these doubts, first attend to and correct any misconceptions that your clients may have about REBT (say, confusing emotional responsibility with self-blame). If these clients still harbour doubts about REBT, suggest they take a 'suck it and see' approach for several sessions. After this trial period, if a few of your clients still retain strong doubts, then a referral to another form of counselling is indicated.

Other clients may have doubts about REBT based on your interactional style (for example, talking too much, adopting the role of a courtroom prosecutor in disputing irrational beliefs) which they assume is the practice of REBT. Investigation may reveal that their objections are aimed at you, not at REBT, which can lead to a modification and improvement in your interactional style which then allows therapy to proceed more smoothly.

The middle stage

As clients move into this stage of counselling, they have usually carried out a few homework tasks and experienced some success in disputing their irrational beliefs. At the same time, however, they begin to see how deeply embedded their irrational beliefs are and how they adversely affect other areas of their life. In a related vein, they find that it is difficult to work in a consistent and determined manner to modify the dysfunctional thinking habits that maintain their emotional problems. Thus, the middle stage of counselling presents you with a number of significant challenges related to promoting therapeutic change. The middle phase of REBT is often called working through (the systematic process of clients giving up their irrational beliefs and internalising a rational outlook). This phase is where most of your time and energy will be spent.

Dealing with multiple problem areas

Typically, your clients will have more than one problem for you to tackle. Sometimes several problems will be listed at the beginning of therapy or, more frequently, new problems will emerge during the course of therapy. This emergence may be due to:

- your clients developing trust in you to the extent that they are now able to reveal problems they previously considered too embarrassing or shameful to discuss;
- your clients developing an awareness of how particular irrational beliefs are adversely affecting a number of different areas of their life; or
- your clients experiencing additional unpleasant activating events during the course of therapy (such as the end of a relationship) that trigger further emotional disturbance.

Ideally, you should work on one problem until the client has achieved a coping criterion and is dealing reasonably well with the problem (Dryden & Neenan, 1995), before moving on to the next one. However, this is not always possible, as some clients will want to focus on another problem before a coping criterion has been attained. When this issue does arise, we suggest you consider the following:

- If you persist in sticking with the original problem, your behaviour might produce an alliance rupture or even termination of therapy (see Chapter 8) as the client interprets your behaviour to mean that your agenda is more important than his.
- When a crisis supervenes (the client loses his job, perhaps, and makes himself depressed through self-blame and self-depreciation), this should become the focus of therapy as it is unlikely that the client's attention will be focused on his original problem (guilt about having an extramarital affair for example). When this crisis has been adequately dealt with (in this case, the client is now looking for another job), therapy can return to the problem that the crisis interrupted.
- Another emotion may emerge (e.g., anger) which interferes with your client's ability to concentrate on his primary emotional problem (e.g., anxiety). It would seem to make little sense to continue to discuss the cognitive structure of anxiety when your client's hot cognitions are related to anger (e.g., 'I shouldn't be anxious!').
- It becomes evident to you that your client has a problem which is not the clinical focus of therapy but pervades many areas of his life, for example dependence on illicit substances which interferes with his functioning at work and interpersonally. This problem could become centre stage if the client agrees that he has a drug problem and is willing to address it (if this problem is outside of your clinical competence, then a referral to a drugs agency is suggested). If the client does not acknowledge there is a problem with illicit drugs, then return to working on the original problem but point out to him the role of illicit drugs in exacerbating this problem if the evidence supports your viewpoint.

Some clients may jump from problem to problem as a form of avoidance behaviour: when emotional pain is experienced, the client moves the discussion to a new, non-threatening topic ('I can't deal with my feelings. I'll be overwhelmed by them'). To tackle this problem, Beck et al. suggest 'dysphoria practice':

> Build[ing] tolerance for dysphoria and to erode patients' dysfunctional beliefs about experiencing uncomfortable situations. To desensitize patients, a hierarchy may be constructed that outlines increasingly painful topics to be discussed in therapy. The therapist can elicit patients' predictions of what they fear will happen before they discuss each succeeding topic, test out the predictions, and accumulate evidence to contradict their faulty beliefs. (1990: 271)

Dysphoria practice can be carried out within the session and as homework assignments.

Identifying core irrational beliefs

As you work on situation-specific irrational beliefs with your clients, you are advised to look for themes among these beliefs which will help you to detect the possible presence of core irrational beliefs. For example, a client who procrastinates over a career change, stays in a relationship he is bored with, goes to the same holiday destination each year and pursues hobbies that no longer excite him may believe, 'I must be absolutely certain that if I change things in my life they will work out well for me because it will be awful if they don't.' You can present your hypotheses regarding core beliefs to your clients for their consideration (remember that a hypothesis is open to disconfirmation, so do not present yours as if it is a fact).

If your client has uncovered a core irrational belief ('I must have the approval of others and it is awful when I don't have it') then a core rational belief needs to be constructed to challenge the irrational belief in every situation that it is operative ('I very much want the approval of others but there is no reason why I must have it. If I don't receive approval it is unfortunate but certainly not awful'). Remember that a core rational belief develops through the client putting himself in real-life situations where he can expect to be disapproved of (following on from the above example); it is not instantly formed in the safety of your office.

It is unlikely that all of your clients' problems will be attributable to a single core irrational belief. In our experience, it is typically two or three core beliefs that underlie clients' problems and usually involve both ego and discomfort disturbance. During the middle stage of therapy, these core beliefs can receive more attention with respect to therapeutic exploration. When core beliefs are identified, you and your client can work on a number of problems concurrently rather than consecutively, which is the case with situation-specific beliefs.

Helping your clients understand how they perpetuate their core irrational beliefs

Educating your clients about the role of core irrational beliefs helps them to see how these beliefs hold sway in their lives. There are three ways in which clients perpetuate their core irrational beliefs:

1 Maintenance of core irrational beliefs – this refers to ways of thinking and acting that perpetuate core beliefs. For example, a person who sees himself as unlikeable refuses invitations to parties, does not initiate social contact, and agrees with the unkind comments of others: his self-imposed social isolation strengthens his negative self-image.
2 Avoidance of core irrational beliefs – this refers to the cognitive, behavioural and emotional strategies clients use to avoid activating their core beliefs and the painful affect associated with them. For example, a person steers the conversation with a friend away from talk of rejection and loneliness to avoid triggering his self-image as unloveable. This strategy does not work in the longer term because, through such avoidance, the person reminds himself of his perceived unloveability.
3 Compensation for core irrational beliefs – this refers to behaviours that the person engages in which seem to contradict his core belief. For example, a client who views himself as incompetent takes on many tasks to prove that he is competent but this strategy backfires as he is overwhelmed by his workload. His self-belief of being incompetent is now reinforced.

It is important for you to help your clients understand how they perpetuate their own core beliefs and to assist them in developing robust cognitive, emotive and behavioural strategies to halt and then dismantle the perpetuation process. For example, in point 3 above, the person now realises that trying to prove he is competent just reminds him that he is incompetent when he does not execute tasks successfully or his workload seems insurmountable. Instead of pursuing this strategy any longer, he strives for self-acceptance and thereby stops tying his self-worth to the completion or non-completion of tasks, though he has a strong preference to be task-competent. He now learns to enjoy himself rather than continually prove himself.

Philosophical vs. non-philosophical change

Uprooting rigid musts and shoulds and their extreme derivatives of awfulising, low frustration tolerance and depreciation of self and others is often referred to in REBT as profound and enduring philosophical change (this kind of change is heavily emphasized in REBT literature).

Philosophical change can occur in specific situations, across situations, or pervade the client's life. While philosophical change is the preferred treatment goal, it is not the only goal on offer (see Chapter 2).

If some of your clients are not interested in philosophical change or believe it is beyond their present capabilities to achieve, then focus on non-philosophical change, such as learning relaxation and breathing techniques to combat their panic attacks instead of dropping their safety behaviours to confront and overcome their fears, such as 'I can't stand feeling dizzy or my head spinning.' These clients always have the option of returning to therapy to pursue a philosophical solution if their non-philosophical one has not helped them in any significant way (in the above example, the panic attacks have not diminished).

Encouraging your clients to engage in relevant homework tasks

A primary task for you during the middle stage of counselling is to help your clients reach emotional insight by strengthening their conviction in their new rational beliefs. Emotional insight, not intellectual insight, is likely to lead to significant and enduring emotional and behavioural changes. By the middle stage of counselling it is important that your clients see the role that they can play in promoting the change process through the use of multimodal homework tasks (see Chapter 3). Underpinning these tasks should, ideally, be a philosophy of effort: 'To get the gain, I have to undergo the strain.' Some clients will see the sense in carrying out homework tasks but have doubts about their ability to carry them out. You can respond to these doubts in a number of ways.

First, work collaboratively with your clients to design homework tasks. Do not impose tasks on your clients or 'push' them to carry out tasks you think will be beneficial for them but they are highly reluctant to do: 'Look, why bother working through a hierarchy of your fears? Just face your worst fear immediately and fully. That's the best and quickest way to bring about change.' We would suggest that you gain client compliance for carrying out tasks by working on the principle of 'challenging, but not overwhelming': clients are encouraged to execute assignments not currently engaged in with frequency or ease (challenging) but which are not regarded by them as too difficult or daunting (overwhelming). In the above example, the client chose a task from the middle of her fear hierarchy rather than starting at the bottom of it (her initial desire) or jumping straight to the top of it (her therapist's choice). Point out to your clients that tasks which elicit little discomfort or involve minimal effort are less likely to promote therapeutic change.

Second, session time can be used for rehearsal of client behaviours that will later be enacted *in vivo*, such as assertion training. Rehearsal can help your clients to deal with 'trouble spots' that impair their performance: the demand 'I must get what I want when I stand up for myself' leads the client to feel angry when he imagines not getting what he believes he must have and his new-found assertiveness quickly falters. Dealing with these trouble spots in the session increases the likelihood of successful task completion outside of the session.

Third, to increase the probability of homework being carried out, be specific in your discussions with your clients: when, what time, where, with whom, and how often will your client carry out the task? Specificity concentrates the client's mind on what is actually involved in carrying out the task in a way that vagueness about the task – 'I'll do it sometime next week' – cannot match. As important as carrying out homework tasks, is reviewing them at the beginning of the next session. Not reviewing them, or reviewing them only in a cursory way, suggests to the client that homework is not so important after all. With regard to homework review, keep the following points in mind:

- What learning has your client extracted from the homework? Avoid framing homework as either success or failure.
- Congratulate clients on their success in carrying out their homework whether it was completed or only attempted.
- Identify, challenge and change any beliefs that interfere with homework completion such as, 'I must experience immediate improvement. As this did not occur, why bother with any more homework?'
- Encourage your clients to try the task again if they were not successful at the first attempt or, if successful, to undertake the task again to prove to themselves it was not a fluke or to drive home the point that completing a task on one occasion is not sufficient to internalise a rational belief – many tasks on many occasions are needed to achieve this.

Fourth, assess the basis for therapeutic change as some of your clients may attribute their change to what REBT would view as self-defeating reasons. For example, a client who is rejected, claims that 'I didn't fancy her anyway as she had big ears', but this is a rationalisation rather than the adoption of a rational outlook which would view rejection as not leading to self-rejection or depreciation of self or others, because there is no reason why others must go out with the client on a date.

Dealing with obstacles to change

A number of significant obstacles to change may be encountered during the middle phase of counselling. Some of these obstacles are:

- The recrudescence of their emotional problems leads some clients to believe they will never overcome these problems and therefore they fail to persist in their change efforts. Change needs to be measured in relative terms (some success and some setbacks) instead of absolute terms (the problem is gone forever). Seeing change in relative terms coupled with an attitude of high frustration tolerance (HFT) is likely to bring more successes than setbacks.

- That change can be a strange and disorientating experience. This state has been called cognitive–emotive dissonance (Maultsby, 1984), meaning it is created by the clash or tension between old and new ways of thinking, feeling and behaving. An example of cognitive–emotive dissonance is the 'I won't be me' syndrome (Grieger & Boyd, 1980): 'If I give up worrying about things, then I won't know who I am any more. I know it sounds silly but worry is part of me. I'll be losing part of me if I change.' You can encourage your clients to accept such feelings as being a natural part of the change process and, if necessary, you can dispute clients' irrational demands to feel natural and comfortable all of the time.

- That some clients, usually a minority, project a false or pretended acceptance of REBT; in other words, they are pseudo-rational. These clients are often erudite in the theory and practice of REBT and provide the 'correct' answers to your questions. However, this REBT knowledge is not put into daily practice and thereby emotional insight is not achieved – rational principles remain in the client's head instead of being acted upon, and knowledge is not translated into belief. Clients who display pseudo-rationality may genuinely believe that intellectual insight alone is sufficient to promote therapeutic change or they may adhere to a philosophy of low frustration tolerance and, therefore, are reluctant to work hard to effect real change in their lives. In each case, challenging and changing these attitudes will help such clients to internalise the REBT view of genuine rationality.

- That clients with perfectionist styles of thinking are often reluctant to surrender their musts because they see them as the motivating force behind their drive for success in life. To give up their musts would mean a decline into mediocrity and inertia (a living death in some clients' minds). You can point out to these clients that powerful desires rather than absolute demands are sufficiently motivating to reach their goals and, as things stand, their perfectionist beliefs bring little real success or enjoyment in their life. As Hauck observes: 'The upshot is that perfectionists achieve near-perfection at great cost to themselves, or achieve far less than those persons who only want perfection' (1980: 140). Perfectionism can lead to anxiety about failure, depression when it occurs, and avoidance of future effort. If clients do descend into mediocrity and inertia through adopting a rational outlook, then they can always return to their old beliefs to reverse this decline (holding open the option of a return to previous ways of functioning can often encourage clients to experiment with change).

Obstacles to change and ways to overcome them were presented from three different perspectives – client, therapist and client–therapist – in Chapters 6, 7 and 8 respectively.

Encouraging clients to maintain and enhance their therapeutic gains

It is usually the case that your clients will experience the greatest variability in their progress during the middle stage of counselling. They will, at times, appear to make significant gains with respect to approaching emotional insight into their problems and then slip back into self-defeating patterns of thinking, feeling and behaving. During this stage, you will need to help your clients deal with their setbacks, maintain the progress they have made, and explore ways to enhance their therapeutic gains. Ellis (1984) has written a pamphlet on these issues which can be summarised as remembering and implementing the three main REBT insights as the mainstay of client progress and looking for, and disputing, rigid musts and shoulds that have 'sneaked back' into clients' thinking when backsliding occurs.

Generalising psychotherapeutic change

Once your client has made headway in effecting psychotherapeutic change on a specific example of his target problem – the problem the client has targeted for change, such as anxiety about being rejected by women – he can take what he has learned and apply it to other examples of his target problem. For example, if your client has made some headway in overcoming his anxiety about being rejected when asking women to dance (a specific example of his target problem), he can then apply what he has learned to other examples of his target problem (such as asking women out for a date). Once he has made progress on this issue, he can then move on to dealing with his fear of being rebuffed when making amorous advances to women (a third example of his target problem). In the majority of cases, clients prefer to tackle a less threatening example of their target problem first, although this is not universally the case and a good principle here is to proceed at an agreed, healthy pace for your client.

The next way in which your client can generalise his therapeutic gains is to apply what he has learned to other situations in which his theme operates: rejection in the case of the client under consideration. Thus, having made progress in dealing with his anxiety about being rejected by women, your client can then generalise what he has learned to other situations in which he fears rejection, for example taking risks at work and dealing with his anxiety about having his ideas rejected, and then moving on to sending his poems to a publisher and risk having them rejected. In this way, your client generalises what he has learned and learns to make himself less vulnerable to rejection.

A further way in which your client can generalise his therapeutic gains is to apply what he has learned and achieved in dealing with the theme of rejection to other themes where he has problems. Thus, your client may have problems in the areas (themes) of success/failure and 'being let down'. If so, he may tackle specific situations in which he is afraid of failing, and apply what he has learned in dealing with rejection to dealing with failure. This application of previous learning is made easier if the two themes reflect similar beliefs in similar areas of disturbance (such as both ego disturbance or non-ego disturbance). However, if your client is trying to generalise from an ego theme to a non-ego theme, he may require more input from you on tackling issues where he is not yet competent as a problem-solver if he is to transfer his psychotherapeutic gains successfully from one theme to the other.

Becoming psychologically healthy

A more ambitious area in which your client can generalise his gains is where he endeavours to apply what he has learned in dealing with problems related to one or more themes to all areas in his life where he disturbs himself. Most clients will need a lot of input from you in order to be able to do this. However, a minority of clients are able to pick up the skills fairly quickly and to assess their problems, dispute their disturbance-producing beliefs and act on their rational beliefs, and can apply these skills successfully whenever they disturb themselves, or are likely to. Such clients tend to make great strides in a relatively short period of time.

Becoming more self-actualising

Reviewing contributions to his edited book on goals in psychotherapy, Mahrer (1967) concluded that there are two basic goals of psychotherapy: overcoming psychological disturbance and promoting self-actualisation. In REBT, we hold the view that it is important to help clients make progress in overcoming their disturbed feelings in a specific problem area or areas before helping them along the path to self-actualisation in that area or those areas. We also hold that the skills which clients need to overcome their emotional disturbance are largely different from the skills they need to acquire in order to pursue self-actualisation. Progress they have made in the former area, therefore, will not necessarily help them make progress in the latter area. Given this fact, do not expect your client to naturally generalise his gains in becoming psychologically healthier to what will be required of him in the area of self-actualisation. You will need to teach him relevant skills if you are to start him along the path towards self-actualisation, a topic that lies outside the scope of this book.

Encouraging your clients to become their own counsellors

During the beginning stage of REBT, you are usually quite active–directive in teaching your clients the ABCs of REBT. In the middle stage, you need to reduce your active–directiveness and encourage your clients to take more of the lead in directing therapy. 'More of the lead' means clients using the ABCDE model to understand and ameliorate their emotional problems assisted by some short Socratic prompts from you to promote independent thought and decrease their dependence on your problem-solving skills. ('What happened at A?' 'How did you feel at C?' 'What were you most upset about in that situation?' 'What did you tell yourself in order to feel that way?' 'How did you dispute that must?' 'What was your rational alternative to the must?' 'What has been the effect on your mood of your rational belief?') If you still rely on didactic teaching to transmit REBT ideas, then you are still doing most of the work of therapy and retarding your clients' progress towards becoming their own therapist.

Some of your clients may not respond well to a decrease in your level of active–directiveness – a client may be prone to form a dependent relationship with you because he has doubts about striking out alone as his own counsellor. You can attempt to deal with this issue by, for example, making reference to prior instances of his successful problem-solving and the obvious point that you will not be there to guide him when therapy ends. If your client is genuinely stuck with resolving a particular problem, you can temporarily become more active–directive until therapeutic movement occurs and then gradually return responsibility to him for dealing with his problem. When your clients respond successfully to your decreased directiveness over several sessions, this can signal that therapy can now move towards termination.

The ending stage

Termination in REBT is not a drawn-out affair. The last few sessions are not essentially different from the ones before and 'the ones near the middle of therapy, except for a somewhat greater emphasis on anticipation of future problems and less emphasis on grappling with present problems' (Wessler & Wessler, 1980: 181).

Relapse prevention

This strategy helps your clients identify those situations (say negative emotional states or interpersonal strife) that could trigger a lapse or relapse into their problems after therapy has ended, and teaches them coping strategies to deal successfully with these situations. As Beck et al. observe: 'Individuals faced with high-risk situations must respond with coping responses. Those who have effective coping responses develop increased self-efficacy, resulting in a decreased probability of relapse' (1993: 11). Relapse prevention in REBT will obviously be based on the skills clients have learnt from you. It is important to build these coping skills in to your treatment plan as 'outcome is increasingly measured not only by treatment success but by relapse prevention' (Padesky & Greenberger, 1995: 70).

It is important to teach your clients the difference between a lapse (stumble) and a relapse (collapse) and that the former state does not inevitably lead to the latter state if they intervene early enough to 'halt the slide'. Some of your clients may express irritation that relapse prevention is even being discussed as it injects into the end – or near-end – of therapy a sour or pessimistic note: 'What's the point of working hard in therapy when you really believe I will be going back to square one when therapy is finished?' Given REBT's view of our seemingly limitless ability to disturb ourselves about anything in our lives, relapse prevention would seem a realistic strategy to pursue. However, the term 'prevention' seems to offer more than it can probably deliver as it suggests we can stop a full-blown recurrence of the original problem. Maybe the term 'relapse reduction' better describes the post-therapy progress of fallible human beings.

When to end

If your clients have made progress in addressing their emotional problems they should be close to termination because they have:

1   internalized a rational philosophy of living and have thereby made reductions in the frequency, duration and intensity of their presenting emotional problems;
2   successfully applied REBT to their presenting problems as well as other problem areas in their lives;
3   identified, challenged and changed core irrational beliefs;
4   developed competence and confidence in acting as a self-therapist;
5   agreed with you that termination is near because the evidence supports this view (persistent hard work has paid off).

However, the reality is that only a few clients usually meet the above criteria for termination. Other clients will, for example, terminate therapy as soon as they experience symptomatic relief from their problems instead of philosophical change about them (for example, a client feels better because his relationship with his partner has improved, instead of focusing on and modifying his underlying belief, 'If she leaves me, which she must not do, then my life will be awful and I'll be worthless') – his fear of being unwanted and abandoned has been deactivated for the time being but is ready to be reactivated when further strains are evident in the relationship. Some clients will only want to challenge and change their situation-specific irrational beliefs, thereby limiting the generalisability of their therapeutic gains.

You can always put the case for wider philosophical change, whether situationally or cross-situationally based, in order for your clients to make themselves much less emotionally disturbable, but never undisturbable. Of course, the final decision regarding termination rests with your clients.

On the other hand, some clients may wish to continue counselling beyond the point of what you consider to be further usefulness. This may occur because these clients believe they need your continuing help in order to maintain their counselling gains or they do not want to lose the special relationship they have developed with you. In the former case, you can devise experiments to test your clients' fears of striking out alone in areas of their lives where they believe they cannot currently cope; while in the latter case, you can explore the feelings that your clients may experience (such as intense sadness) about the end of the relationship ('If you see the relationship as special, then it will be a significant loss to you but not an awful one').

You may be unwilling to terminate counselling with clients who have shown considerable progress and/or you especially like. You may believe that continued evidence of these clients' progress means you are a competent practitioner and a worthwhile person, while keeping especially likeable clients in therapy provides you with relief from the dull, ordinary, difficult or unlikeable clients that mostly fill your caseload. Needless to say, your irrational beliefs underpinning these two problems should be examined.

You can suggest to your clients that follow-up appointments can be arranged to monitor their progress and they can contact you if they encounter prolonged difficulties in practising REBT.

In this book, we have shown you the REBT view of psychotherapeutic change: understanding and implementing the ABCDE model of psychological disturbance and change (primarily philosophical change); understanding the respective roles of client and therapist in promoting change for the former; dealing with obstacles to change that inhibit client progress; and, finally, following the process of change through the beginning, middle and terminating stages of therapy and beyond.

References

Beck, A. T., Freeman, A. & Associates (1990). *Cognitive therapy of personality disorders.* New York: Guilford.

Beck, A. T., Wright, F. D., Newman, C. F., & Liese, B. S. (1993). *Cognitive therapy of substance abuse.* New York: Guilford.

Bernard, M. E., & Wolfe, J. L. (Eds.) (2000). *The REBT resource book for practitioners.* New York: Albert Ellis Institute.

Bond, F. W., & Dryden, W. (1996). Why two, central REBT hypotheses appear untestable. *Journal of Rational-Emotive & Cognitive-Behavior Therapy, 14*, 29–40.

Bordin, E. S. (1979). The generalizability of the psychoanalytic concept of the working alliance. *Psychotherapy: Theory, Research and Practice, 16*, 252–260.

Bruch, M., & Bond, F. W. (Eds.) (1998). *Beyond diagnosis: case formulation approaches in CBT.* Chichester: Wiley.

Burns, D. D. (1989). *The feeling good handbook.* New York: William Morrow.

DiGiuseppe, R. (1988). Thinking what to feel. In W. Dryden & P. Trower (Eds.), *Developments in rational-emotive therapy* (pp. 22–29). Milton Keynes: Open University Press.

DiGiuseppe, R. (1991). Comprehensive cognitive disputing in RET. In M. E. Bernard (Ed.), *Using rational-emotive therapy effectively: a practitioner's guide* (pp. 173–195). New York: Plenum.

Dowd, E. T. (1996). Resistance and reactance in cognitive therapy. *International Cognitive Therapy Newsletter, 10* (3), 3–5.

Dryden, W. (1986). Vivid methods in rational-emotive therapy. In A. Ellis & R. M. Grieger (Eds.), *Handbook of rational-emotive therapy. Volume 2* (pp. 221–245). New York: Springer.

Dryden, W. (Ed.) (1990). *The essential Albert Ellis.* New York: Springer.

Dryden, W. (1995). *Preparing for client change in rational emotive behaviour therapy.* London: Whurr.

Dryden, W. (1998). Understanding persons in the context of their problems: a rational emotive behaviour therapy perspective. In M. Bruch & F. W. Bond (Eds.), *Beyond diagnosis: case formulation approaches in CBT* (pp. 43–64). Chichester: Wiley.

Dryden, W. (1999). *Rational emotive behaviour therapy: a personal approach.* Bicester: Winslow.

Dryden, W. (2001). *Reason to change: a rational emotive behaviour therapy (REBT) workbook.* Hove: Brunner/Routledge.

Dryden, W., & Neenan, M. (1995). *Dictionary of rational emotive behaviour therapy.* London: Whurr.

Dryden, W., Neenan, M., & Yankura, J. (1999). *Counselling individuals: a rational emotive behavioural handbook* (3rd ed.). London: Whurr.

Ellis, A. (1959). Requisite conditions for basic personality change. *Journal of Consulting Psychology, 23,* 538–540.

Ellis, A. (1963). Toward a more precise definition of 'emotional' and 'intellectual' insight. *Psychological Reports, 13,* 125–126.

Ellis, A. (1978). Personality characteristics of rational-emotive therapists and other kinds of therapists. *Psychotherapy: Theory, Research and Practice, 15,* 329–332.

Ellis, A. (1984). *How to maintain and enhance your rational-emotive therapy gains.* New York: Albert Ellis Institute.

Ellis, A. (1985). *Overcoming resistance.* New York: Springer.

Ellis, A. (1994). *Reason and emotion in psychotherapy* (revised and updated ed.). New York: Birch Lane Press.

Ellis, A. (2001). Rational and irrational aspects of countertransference. *Journal of Clinical Psychology/In Session: Psychotherapy in Practice, 57,* 999–1004.

Ellis, A. (2002). *Overcoming resistance: a rational emotive therapy integrated approach* (second ed.). New York: Springer.

Ellis, A., McInerney, J. F., DiGiuseppe, R., & Yeager, R. J. (1988). *Rational-emotive therapy with alcoholics and substance abusers.* New York: Pergamon.

Glover, M. (1988). Responsibility and therapy. In W. Dryden & P. Trower (Eds.), *Developments in cognitive psychotherapy* (pp. 106–127). London: Sage Publications.

Golden, W. L., & Dryden, W. (1986). Cognitive-behavioural therapies: commonalities, divergences and future developments. In W. Dryden & W. L. Golden (Eds.), *Cognitive-behavioural approaches to psychotherapy* (pp. 356–378). London: Harper & Row.

Grieger, R. M. (1991). Keys to effective RET. In M. E. Bernard (Ed.), *Using rational-emotive therapy effectively: a practitioner's guide.* New York: Plenum.

Grieger, R., & Boyd, J. (1980). *Rational-emotive therapy: a skills-based approach.* New York: Van Nostrand Reinhold.

Hanna, F. J. (2002). *Therapy with difficult clients.* Washington, DC: American Psychological Association.

Hauck, P. (1966). The neurotic agreement in psychotherapy. *Rational Living, 1*(1), 32–35.

Hauck, P. (1980). *Brief counseling with RET.* Philadelphia, PA: Westminster Press.

Hauck, P. (1991). *Hold your head up high.* London: Sheldon Press.

Kwee, M. G. T., & Lazarus, A. A. (1986) Multimodal therapy: the cognitive-behavioural tradition and beyond. In W. Dryden and W. L. Golden (Eds.), *Cognitive-behavioural approaches to psychotherapy* (pp. 320–335). London: Harper & Row.

Lazarus, A. A. (1989). *The practice of multimodal therapy* (updated paperback ed.). Baltimore, MD: The Johns Hopkins University Press.

Lazarus, A. A., & Lazarus, C. N. (1991). *Multimodal life history inventory.* Champaign, IL: Research Press.

Leahy, R. L. (2001). *Overcoming resistance in cognitive therapy.* New York: Guilford.

Ludgate, J. W. (1995). *Maximizing psychotherapeutic gains and preventing relapse in emotionally distressed clients.* Sarasota, FL: Professional Resource Press.

Mahrer, A. R. (Ed.) (1967). *The goals of psychotherapy.* New York: Appleton-Century-Crofts.

Maultsby, M. C., Jr. (1984). *Rational behavior therapy.* Englewood Cliffs, NJ: Prentice-Hall.

Neenan, M., & Dryden, W. (1996). *Dealing with difficulties in rational emotive behaviour therapy*. London: Whurr.

Neenan, M., & Dryden, W. (2000). *Essential rational emotive behaviour therapy*. London: Whurr.

Neenan, M., & Dryden, W. (2001). *Learning from errors in rational emotive behaviour therapy*. London: Whurr.

Neenan, M., & Dryden, W. (2002). *Cognitive behaviour therapy: an A–Z of persuasive arguments*. London: Whurr.

Padesky, C. A., & Greenberger, D. (1995). *Clinician's guide to mind over mood*. New York: Guilford.

Persons, J. B. (1989). *Cognitive therapy in practice: a case formulation approach*. New York: Norton.

Rogers, C. R. (1957). The necessary and sufficient conditions of therapeutic personality change. *Journal of Consulting Psychology, 21*, 459–461.

Safran, J. D., & Muran, J. C. (2000). *Negotiating the therapeutic alliance*. New York: Guilford.

Salkovskis, P. M. (1996). The cognitive approach to anxiety: threat beliefs, safety-seeking behavior, and the special case of health anxiety and obsessions. In P. M. Salkovskis (Ed.), *Frontiers of cognitive therapy*. New York: Guilford.

Teasdale, J. D. (1996). Clinically relevant theory: integrating clinical insight with cognitive science. In P. M. Salkovskis (Ed.), *Frontiers of cognitive therapy*. New York: Guilford.

Teasdale, J. D., & Barnard, P. J. (1993). *Affect, cognition and change: re-modelling depressive thought*. Hillsdale, NJ: Lawrence Erlbaum Associates.

Walen, S. R., DiGiuseppe, R., & Dryden, W. (1992). *A practitioner's guide to rational-emotive therapy* (2nd ed.). New York: Oxford University Press.

Walker, M. (1993). When values clash. In W. Dryden (Ed.), *Questions and answers on counselling in action*. London: Sage Publications.

Wessler, R. A., & Wessler, R. L. (1980). *The principles and practice of rational-emotive therapy*. San Francisco, CA: Jossey-Bass.

Yapp, R., & Dryden, W. (1994). Supervision in REBT: the thirteen step self-supervision inventory. *The Rational Emotive Behaviour Therapist, 2* (1), 16–24.

Index

Page numbers in *italics* refer to figures.

ABC model
  As (actual or inferred events) 5–7
  Bs (beliefs) 7–11
  Cs (consequences of beliefs) 11–13,
    14, 15
  teaching the client 59–60, 123–5
ABCDE model 51, 134
acceptance
  avoiding judgemental attitude 104–5
  of problem 35–6
  of role of beliefs 36
  self-acceptance 60–1
  unconditional 47–8, 60–1, 109–10, 122
  vs. deprecation beliefs 10–11, 87, 95
acceptance of responsibility
  emotional 72–3
  psychological 36, 57–8, 72–3
  therapeutic 73–4
active–directive approach 2–3, 51,
  110–11, 122, 134
  vs. passivity 98–9
actual behaviours/action tendencies
  12, *14*
actual or inferred events (As) 5–7
anger
  healthy vs. unhealthy 21–3, 53–4
  therapist 95–6, 97
  see also low vs. high frustration
    tolerance; resentment
approval needs, therapist 95
arguing with clients 97
assessment 62, 68
audiotaping sessions 55, 62, 94
'authentic chameleon' 100
authoritative role of therapist 49
avoidance of core irrational beliefs 128
awfulising beliefs
  and validation 112
  vs. non-awfulising beliefs 8–9, 85–6

Beck, A.T. et al. 114, 127, 134–5
beginning stage of change 121–5

beginning the therapeutic relationship
  56, 121–3
behavioural–cognitive dissonance 83
behavioural change 2, 25–7, 31–2
behavioural consequences of beliefs 12
behavioural goal 38
behavioural skills 27
behaviour(s)
  interactions 1–2
  rehearsal of 129–30
  safety-seeking 26–7, 82
belief–action consistency 43
belief–behaviour–thinking configurations
  64–5
belief change 2–3, 23, 27–9, 34
  continuum 33
  facilitating other types of change 30–3
  qualitative vs. quantitative view 41
  self-debate 73–4
beliefs (Bs)
  ABC model 7–11
  characteristics 7–8
  client acceptance of role of 36
  consequences of (Cs) 11–13, *14, 15*
  types 8–11
  see also entries beginning irrational;
    rational
Bernard, M.E. and Wolfe, J.L. 55
Bond, F.W.
  Bruch, M. and 62
  and Dryden, W. 12–13
bonds 121–2
Bordin, E. 4, 47, 53, 121
Bruch, M. and Bond, F.W. 62

caring too much 103
change goals *see* goal(s)
change obstacles and solutions 66, 130–2
  client 80–92
  client–therapist 108–20
  therapist 93–107
change roles
  client 35–6, 67–79
  therapist 46–66

change sequence 35–45
change stages
    beginning 121–5
    ending 134–6
    middle 125–34
change types 17–34
cognitions
    importance of 1
    interactions 1–2
cognitive–behavioural dissonance 83
cognitive–emotive dissonance 77, 131
cognitive change 2, 54
cognitive consequences of beliefs
        12–13, 15
cognitive goals 38, 54
collaboration 69–70, 129
collaborative empiricism 48, 49
commitment to change 38–9, 44–5, 69
communicator credibility 52
compensation/overcompensation 82, 128
complacency 87
congruence
    goal 123
    in therapeutic relationship 48
consequences of beliefs (Cs) 11–13, 14, 15
constructive vs. dysfunctional
        behaviour 25–6
cost–benefit analysis 84
countertransference issues 115–16
critical As 6–7
    distracting oneself from 21
    facing and focusing on 63
    inferential change 17–20

decreasing contact principle 58
'demand' characteristics of REBT 67
demands vs. non-dogmatic preferences 8
denial 81–2
deprecation vs. acceptance beliefs
        10–11, 87, 95
DiGiuseppe, R. 35, 40
discomfort of change 91–2
dislike of client 112–14
distracting oneself from critical As 21
doubts see reservations
Dowd, E.T. 101
Dryden, W. 4, 36, 41, 42, 62, 63, 101–2, 124
    Bond, F.W. and 12–13
    Golden, W.L. and 111
    and Neenan, M. 126
    Neenan, M. and 70, 80, 102, 109, 124
    Yapp, R. and 55, 62
dysfunctional vs. constructive behaviour
        25–6
'dysphoria practice' 127

educator role 50, 59–61, 63
    ABC model 59–60, 123–5
    lecturing too much 98
    putting words into client's mouth 99–100
    self-therapy skills 134
Ellis, A. 1–4, 8, 40, 41, 51, 52, 59, 75, 76, 80,
        96–7, 98, 106, 113, 115, 132
emotional change 2, 32–3, 37, 53–4
emotional consequences of beliefs 11–12
emotional goal 37, 53–4
emotional insight 41–3
    vs. intellectual insight 40–1, 87–8, 131
emotional responsibility 72–3
emotions
    interactions 1–2
    meta-emotional problems 74, 122–3
    negative 11–12, 13, 14, 15
    qualitative vs. quantitative view 11–12
    validation/ventilation of 110–12
emotive–cognitive dissonance 77, 131
empathy 47
    limitations 111
    vs. problem–solving 110–11
encouragement 49–50, 63–5, 129–30, 132
    self-help 57–8, 134
ending stage of change 134–6
ending the therapeutic relationship 58–9
Epictetus 1, 36, 70, 124
experiential learning 26

follow-up appointments 136
force and energy 43
freedom of choice 108–10

generalising therapeutic gains 63–5, 132–3
genuineness 48
Glover, M. 109–10
goal(s)
    behavioural 38
    client attainment 49
    client commitment 38–9
    client identification 36–8
    client recognition 39–40
    client reservations 83–4
    client vs. therapist 103–4
    cognitive 38
    congruence 123
    domain of working relationship 53–4
    emotional 37
    maintaining focus 57
    selection 71–2, 122–3
Golden, W.L. and Dryden, W. 111
Grieger, R. and Boyd, J. 68–9, 77, 111, 131
Grieger, R.M. 69
guilt 54

Hauck, P. 60, 73, 93, 103, 131
here and now focus 68–9
high frustration tolerance *see* low vs. high
    frustration tolerance (LFT/HFT)
highly reactive clients 100, 101
histrionic clients 100, 101
homework assignments 75–6, 129–30
    see also self-help

'I won't be me' syndrome 131
ICS model *see* interactive cognitive
    systems model
identifying core irrational beliefs 127
imagery, use of 65
inappropriate self-disclosure 96–7
inferences 11–12, *13*, 60
inferential change 17–20, 23–5, 30–1
inferred or actual events (As) 5–7
intellectual clients 100, 101–2
intellectual insight 40–1, 74–5
    vs. emotional insight 40–1, 87–8, 131
interactive cognitive systems (ICS)
    model 41
interdependence principle of change 33–4
interpersonal style conflicts 100–2, 125
irrational beliefs
    identifying 127
    pacing challenge to 105
    perpetuating 128
    therapist–client 93–4
    see also entries beginning belief; rational

judgemental attitude 104–5

'know nothingness' 118–19
Kwee, M.G.T. and Lazarus, A.A. 100

lapses 49–50
    vs. relapse 135
Lazarus, A.A. 51
    Kwee, M.G.T. and 100
    and Lazarus, C.N. 101
'laziness' 90–1
Leahy, R.L. 110, 112, 115
lecturing too much 98
lifetime commitment to change 44–5
low vs. high frustration tolerance
    (LFT/HFT) 9–10, 86–7, 90–2
    therapist 106–7, 118–19
    see also anger; resentment
Ludgate, J.W. 44

Mahrer, A.R. 133
maintenance
    of core irrational beliefs 128

maintenance *cont.*
    of therapeutic gains 44–5, 78–9, 132
    of therapeutic relationship 56–8
Maultsby Jr., M.C. 57, 88, 131
mental rehearsal of rational beliefs 43, 63–5
meta-emotional problems 74, 122–3
metacommunication 119
middle stage of change 125–34
motivation
    client vs. therapist 106
    decreased 85
multiple problem areas 125–7
mutual attraction 117–18

narcissistic traits 89–90
Neenan, M.
    and Dryden, W. 70, 80, 102, 109, 124
    Dryden, W. and 126
negative emotions 11–12, *13, 14, 15*
neurotic agreement, therapist–client 93–4
non-awfulising vs. awfulising beliefs
    8–9, 85–6
non-critical inferred As 6, 7
non-dogmatic preferences
    and decreased motivation 85
    vs. demands 8
non-linear process of change 44

obstacles *see* change obstacles and
    solutions; reservations; resistance
open-mindedness 71–2
over-excitable clients 100, 101
overcoming psychological problems
    (OPP) goals 71–2
overcompensation/compensation 82, 128

pace of therapy 52, 102, 106–7
Padesky, C.A. and Greenberger, D. 114, 135
passivity
    client 100, 101
    therapist 98–9
perfectionist clients 131
persistence
    client 43
    therapist 106–7
personal development (PD) goals 71–2
personal dislike of client 112–14
personal life, therapist 116–17
personal style, client 100–2
Persons, J.B. 62, 96
philosophical vs. non-philosophical
    change 128–9
philosophy of effort 75
    see also protestant work ethic
power games 95–6

presenting problem
  describing 68
  identifying core irrational beliefs 127
prevention of relapse 44, 57, 65–6,
  78, 134–5
principles of REBT 1–4
problem-solving vs. empathy 110–11
propaganda, external and internal 2–3
protestant work ethic 4, 55
  see also philosophy of effort
pseudo-rationality 131
psychological educator see educator role
psychological interactionism 1–2,
  16, 33–4
psychological responsibility 36,
  57–8, 72–3
putting words into client's mouth
  99–100

qualitative vs. quantitative view
  of belief change 41
  of emotions 11–12

rational beliefs
  rehearsal 43, 63–5
  reservations 84–7
  techniques 41–3
rational judo 42
rational portfolio technique 42
rational principles, teaching 60–1
'rational therapy' 1
realistic egalitarianism 50–1
reality-testing 71
referral 110–11, 114, 125
rehearsal
  of behaviours 129–30
  of rational beliefs 43, 63–5
relapse prevention 44, 57, 65–6,
  78, 134–5
remorse 54
repetition technique 42
resentment, therapist 119–20
reservations
  freedom of choice 108–10
  goals for change 83–4
  'I can't change' obstacle 80–1
  rational beliefs 84–7
  REBT model 125
resignation 87
resistance
  interpersonal style conflicts 100–2, 125
  neglecting homework assignments
    89–91
  pacing interventions 105
  understanding and overcoming 76

responsibility see acceptance of
  responsibility
reviewing homework tasks 130
Rogers, C. 3, 4, 47

safety-seeking behaviour 26–7, 82
Safran, J.D. and Muran, J.C.
  108–9, 119
Salkovskis, P.M. 26
self-acceptance, unconditional 60–1
self-actualising skills 133
self-debate 73–4
self-disclosure 48
  inappropriate 96–7
self-esteem 60
self-help
  encouragement 57–8, 134
  forms 55
  misunderstanding of concept 88–9
  obstacles to 88–91
  see also homework assignments
self-therapy skills 63, 77–8, 133, 134
self-worth, therapist 95–6
sexual attraction 117–18
shame 81, 82
shared irrational beliefs 93–4
short-term 'solutions' 81–3
situational As 6, 7
  changing 21–5
skills
  behavioural 27
  self-actualising 133
  self-therapy 63, 77–8, 133, 134
  therapist 55, 62
SMART goal selection 71–2, 122
sociotrophic clients 100, 101
structuring the therapeutic process 61
supervision, therapist 55, 62, 94, 113

task(s)
  client-therapist 123
  completions, encouragement for 49
  domain of working relationship 54–5
teaching see educator role
Teasdale, J.D. and Barnard, P.J. 41
therapeutic conditions 3, 4
therapeutic relationship 3–4
  core conditions 47–8
  interpersonal style conflicts
    100–2, 125
  obstacles to change 108–20
  see also working relationship
therapeutic responsibility 73–4
therapeutic role 48–51
therapeutic style 51–2

time factors
  lifetime commitment to change 44–5
  pace of therapy 52, 102, 106–7
  self-help 89
tolerance
  for dysphoria 127
  of uncertainty 77
  see also low vs. high frustration
    tolerance (LFT/HFT)
transference issues 114–16

uncertainty 77
unconditional acceptance 47–8, 109–10, 122
unconditional self-acceptance 60–1
'understanding of the person in the context
  of his problems' (UPCP) 62
unfamiliarity of change 91–2
unrealistic expectations, therapist 102–3

validation/ventilation of emotions
  110–12

Walen, S.R. et al. 97, 99, 116
Walker, M. 112
Wessler, R.A. and Wessler, R.L. 23–5,
  95–6, 102–3, 134
work ethic (protestant ethic) 4, 55
  see also philosophy of effort
working relationship 4, 46–7, 52–5
  beginning 56, 121–3
  collaborative 48, 49, 69–70, 129
  ending 58–9
  maintaining 56–8
  realistic egalitarianism 50–1
  see also therapeutic relationship

Yapp, R. and Dryden, W. 55, 62